Are UFOs real? Are they the key to unlocking the door to immortality, freedom, and peace? You are invited to take a journey into another dimension of time and space and discover the shocking truth behind the origin of "close encounters." You'll understand why there is such a resurgence of interest in UFOs. Most important, you'll find out how you can experience a close encounter of the *infinite kind* and how to open the door to true immortality!

Infinite Encounters

Frank Allnutt

SPIRE BOOKS

Fleming H. Revell Company
Old Tappan, New Jersey

Special appreciation is given to John Veitch, vice president of Columbia Pictures, and Marvin Levy, publicist for *Close Encounters of the Third Kind,* for their interest in this book and assistance, without which the book could not have been completed.

Excerpts from the book CLOSE ENCOUNTERS OF THE THIRD KIND by Steven Spielberg. Copyright © 1977 by Columbia Pictures, a division of Columbia Pictures Industries, Inc. Reprinted by permission of DELACORTE PRESS.

Excerpts from the book THE HYNEK UFO REPORT by J. Allen Hynek. Copyright © 1977 by J. Allen Hynek. Reprinted by permission of DELL PUBLISHING CO., INC.

Excerpt from "Unidentified Flying Objects" by Carl Sagan reprinted with permission of The Encyclopedia American, copyright 1977 The Americana Corporation.

Excerpts from THE SPACESHIPS OF EZEKIEL by Josef F. Blumrich. Copyright © 1974 by Econ Verlagsgruppe. By permission of Bantam Books, Inc.

Excerpts from UFO'S: WHAT ON EARTH IS HAPPENING copyright 1975, Harvest House Publishers, 2861 McGaw, Irvine, California 92714.

Excerpts from OPERATION TROJAN HORSE by John Keel copyright © 1970 by G. P. Putnam's Sons. Used by permission.

Excerpt from REPORT ON UNIDENTIFIED FLYING OBJECTS by Capt. E. J. Ruppelt copyright © 1956 by Doubleday & Company, Inc. Used by permission.

Excerpts from CHARIOTS OF THE GODS by Erich Von Daniken copyright © 1971 by G. P. Putnam's Sons. Used by permission.

Excerpt from A THEOLOGY OF THE NEW TESTAMENT by George E. Ladd copyright © 1974 by William B. Eerdmans Publishing Company. Used by permission.

Excerpt from COMMENTARY ON THE BOOK OF REVELATION by George E. Ladd copyright © 1972 by William B. Eerdmans Publishing Company. Used by permission.

Library of Congress Cataloging in Publication Data

Allnutt, Frank.
   Infinite encounters.

   (Spire books)
   1. Flying saucers (in religion, folk-lore, etc.)
I. Title.
TL789.A56   001.9'42   78-9006
ISBN 0-8007-8335-2

This is an original Spire Book, published by Spire Books, a division of Fleming H. Revell Company, Old Tappan, New Jersey

Contents

Preface

Movie critics predict that *Close Encounters of the Third Kind* will rank among the top motion pictures of all time, sharing honors with *Star Wars* and *Jaws*. "It deserves an historic place in movie entertainment," wrote Jack Kroll of *Newsweek*. "Steven Spielberg's giant, spectacular 1970s science-fiction movie is the best—most elaborate—ever made," praised the *New York Times'* Vincent Canby. "*Close Encounters* is, in all probability, the most important film of our time," declared Ray Bradbury in the *Los Angeles Times*.

What is it that makes *Close Encounters* so compelling an attraction? Is it because it is so superior a motion picture? Is it because of the resurgence of interest in UFOs? Yes, these reasons are part of the answer. But, perhaps, Ray Bradbury has hit on the most basic reason for the film's runaway success: "This is a religious film," he wrote. And, indeed, it is a religious film. It's about religion of the new space-age variety—the gospel according to *Close Encounters of the Third Kind*. It tells us that UFOs are real and that they are the key to unlocking the beautiful door to true immortality.

But the film raises many questions over its claims and inferences. Just what are UFOs anyway? Where do they come from? What is their true purpose? Will they really open the door to immortality? Are we to believe that God is a UFOnaut? What does the Bible say about UFOs, God, and immortality?

Some experts, such as astronomer J. Allen Hynek, believe that UFOs exist in a "parallel reality." This book will take you on a journey into that "parallel reality"—that other dimension of time and space—to reveal the shocking truth behind the origin of UFOs and why they are here. More important, this book explains the simple way you can have a close encounter of the infinite kind and open the door to true immortality and enter in.

Infinite Encounters

Part 1
Encountering Close Encounters

1

The Compelling Encounter

Out of the mysterious phenomenon of unidentified flying objects (UFOs) has come one of the most challenging motion pictures ever to be produced, and possibly one of the most entertaining ones ever to be beheld on the screen—*Close Encounters of the Third Kind*. It has exploded upon moviegoing America with no less impact than if alien beings really had dropped out of a billowing cloud at night and made contact with us earthlings.

Wisely booked for exclusive engagements only in Los Angeles and New York before going into general release on December 14, 1977, the movie quickly began drawing multitudes waiting in lines for up to four hours to witness what the movie's makers have called "earth's greatest adventure."

The Light Beyond

Full-page ads appeared in newspapers and intriguing commercials showed up on television. The critics gave the film glowing reviews. *Newsweek* devoted its cover to the film and ran a lengthy review inside.

The word was spreading fast: *Close Encounters of the Third Kind* was a must-see picture.

The Blessings of the Critics

For science-fiction critics, *Close Encounters of the Third Kind,* coupled with *Star Wars,* made the year 1977 a vintage year—if not *the* vintage year for films of their genre. Not since Stanley Kubrick's *2001: A Space Odyssey,* has there been such a year for science-fiction films. Indeed, people flocked to the theaters in droves to see Kubrick's creation, though many admitted it was a rather fuzzy statement on the wretchedness of mankind, whose final option was to escape to the farthest corner of the universe and be reincarnated, not as man, but as naked mind drifting among the stars.

The purists say *2001: A Space Odyssey* was genuine science fiction. Then came 1977 and George Lucas's *Star Wars* (more aptly called science *fantasy*), a delightful rehash of familiar people and themes and symbols, all dressed up in brilliant new technology, spectacular and innovative effects, and new (yet used-looking) space hardware.

Close behind *Star Wars* came Steven Spielberg's *Close Encounters of the Third Kind* (which was billed not as science fiction by its makers, but rather as science *speculation*).

The two things about *Close Encounters* that are so intriguing, so compelling, to so many people are: first, the mounting controversy over the phenomenon of UFOs, and, second, the space-age doctrine that UFOs are an open door to immortality. Evidently, moviegoers and critics, as well, liked

14

the film for both reasons.

One of the most enthusiastic of the movie critics was Ray Bradbury, the well-known science-fiction writer in his own right. Bradbury wrote, *"Close Encounters* knows exactly where the center of the universe is . . . (it) is the science-fiction film we have all been waiting for . . . in all probability, the most important film of our time . . . I dare to predict that in every way, aesthetically or commercially, it will be the most successful film ever produced, released, or seen. It will be the first film in history to gross $1 billion, all by itself" (Ray Bradbury, "Opening the Beautiful Door of True Immortality," *Los Angeles Times*, 20 November 1977, p. 50).

Judging from early, record-breaking results at the box office, it appears that Bradbury's predictions for the success of *Close Encounters* might come true.

Phantom Squadron

Close Encounters begins on an ominous note when a phantom squadron of World War II planes in like-new condition mysteriously turns up in sand-blown Sonoyita in northern Mexico. Just as mysteriously, the pilots of the vintage planes had disappeared more than thirty years ago, without a trace. We quickly get the impression, though, that Frenchman Claude Lacombe (Francois Truffaut), the dedicated expert on extraordinary phenomena who heads an international "silence group" that is seeking a breakthrough in communicating with UFOs, knows much more than meets the eye.

Making the Inanimate Animate

The story jumps to evening, and a quiet, peaceful setting in rural Indiana. Like the calm before the

15

storm, you just *know* that at any moment some alien being will jump out of the shadows and scare you plumb silly!

But, instead, Spielberg takes a more subtle, humorous approach. Little three-year-old Barry Guiler (Cary Guffey) is awakened when a UFO beams an activating ray into his toy monkey, causing it to clap its tiny cymbals together. Then, one after another, Barry's other toys become animated, and he toddles from room to room, smiling whimsically at the fantastically amusing show his toys are putting on.

It's almost as if Walt Disney were about to bring Winnie the Pooh to life! (Walt's influence is sensed time and again throughout the film.)

Shades of Mary Poppins

The whole scene is also strikingly reminiscent of the "Spoon Full of Sugar" sequence from Walt Disney's *Mary Poppins*. In the Disney film, the "practically perfect" young English nanny, played by Julie Andrews, mysteriously causes her two young charges' toys, clothes, and bedding to become animated in a demonstration that proved that tidying up the room can be fun! But the animated toys in *Close Encounters* affect us differently, because we *know* that unseen flying saucers are activating them.

Barry's mother, Jillian Guiler (Melinda Dillon), who is on the downhill side of a rough case of the flu, awakens just in time to see her son stroll out of the house and away.

Meanwhile, the hero of *Close Encounters*, Roy Neary (Richard Dreyfuss), a hard-hat suburbanite who works for the Department of Water and Power, is called away from his wife, Ronnie (Teri Garr), and his three kids, to investigate a massive power black-out. He gets lost in the country, then is terrified by a bright UFO that hovers nearby with a deep, deafening roar (the Dolby sound raises *Close Encounters* from entertainment to an *experience*). The UFO somehow causes Roy's DWP truck to first stop running, and then to go completely berserk. Instrument gauges go haywire, and then there's a whirlwind of everything loose in the cab.

Roy Encounters Jillian

The UFO finally departs, and the engine of Roy's now half-wrecked truck starts up by itself. He then intercepts a radio message that the UFO has been spotted nearby. He soon finds himself whizzing down a country highway along with several police cruisers in hot pursuit of a flying saucer! Rounding a curve, Roy barely misses hitting little Barry, who has wandered off from home, but the close call brings Roy and Jillian into a personal encounter.

Little did they know that their brief encounter would be the start of an incredible adventure that would bring them together again at Devil's Tower in Wyoming where the close encounter of the third kind would take place.

The UFOs Return

A couple of nights later, Jillian heard a sound that, at first, she thought was thunder, and then sounded more like a swarm of bees. Then she noticed the clouds were swirling violently, unlike anything she had ever seen before. They began to cast an orange glow from within! Immediately, Jillian knew that the UFOs had come back. Quickly, she ran with Barry and locked themselves inside the house. In moments the contents of the house became animated, just as they had a few nights before—but this time was worse, much worse.

From Whimsey to Violence

What had started as whimsical fun with Barry's toys the other night, now turned into terrifying violence! The kitchen stove began pulsating. Its electrical burners glowed red hot from the UFO's supercharging. The refrigerator opened its doors and spewed out its contents across the floor. The activated TV set blared, and a toy police car, with its tiny siren wailing, cruised the house! Before the episode had ended, the house was in a shambles.

What had begun as delightful UFO fun on the first night in the Guiler household had now escalated into terrifying destruction.

The whole thing was similar to the animated kitchens in Walt Disney's "Carousel of Progress" at the 1963–64 New York World's Fair and Disneyland—but gone crazy!

Some critics likened the scene to the "Sorcerer's Apprentice" sequence in Walt Disney's film classic *Fantasia,* in which Mickey Mouse, as the junior wizard, loses control of the magic energy.

Ordinary People

While Walt Disney tended to place either extraordinary or superficial people in extraordinary circumstances, Spielberg's characters are ordinary and believable people who find themselves engulfed in extraordinary situations. Disney's optimistic fantasy stands in interesting contrast to Spielberg's realistic, humanist one.

"What we admire most about Steven's work," explained co-producer Julia Phillips, "is that he makes movies about people, people with whom audiences can identify. In this one, the principal man is really every man."

The Abduction

The innocence of childhood is exploited to its fullest when little Barry is delightfully and irresistibly drawn outside his house by the eerie light from a beckoning UFO. Jillian tries desperately to hold onto Barry, but he slips from her grasp, and she loses him to the alien abductors.

Wrought with emotion, Jillian tries unsuccessfully to convince everyone of her son's abduction, but, curiously, the authorities don't show much concern about the missing boy's whereabouts.

Roy's sanity is being questioned more and more by his wife, Ronnie. He is obsessed with trying to sculpt the form of some hazy image in his mind. He tries to shape it out of shaving cream, then mashed potatoes, and finally, after losing his job and family, with a mound of dirt and assorted junk and debris in his living room.

Devil's Tower

The excitement level of the film subsides briefly while Spielberg assembles Jillian, Roy, and others at Devil's Tower in Wyoming where the final, unprecedented forty minutes of motion-picture awe and wonder explode in an orchestrated blend of movement, color, light, and reverberant sound.

To Claude Lacombe, the incredible encounter means the culmination of a global search. To Jillian, it means the realization of her hope of finding little Barry. To Roy, it means finding the answer to the irresistible mystery that had driven him to the brink of an emotional breakdown.

For movie audiences, Spielberg has succeeded in making the encounter a spiritually intimate kind of experience—one in which something so ardently longed for by so many people was becoming a reality before their eyes. For some, it proved to be a moment approaching the sublime, if not reverence, for the technical mysticism thrust upon them.

I'm sure that Ray Bradbury must have been weeping with ecstasy, both when he first experienced *Close Encounters* on the screen and, later, when he wrote about it:

"For when the moment arrives at the end of this film when the greatest Encounter ever occurs, we feel one door of Time close for once and all, and the finest, most beautiful door, the door of true immortality, open upon tomorrow and tomorrow and tomorrow. Suddenly we can see ourselves reflected and rereflected down and out along Time without diminution, without exhaustion.

"The thing we have prayed for, thought of at three in the morning, wanted at dawn, hoped for on some winter afternoon when the sun went down at two o'clock, has finally arrived into our hands—to encounter Forever and know it, own it, be it.

"With Spielberg's extraterrestrial Visitors, traveling to blueprint/star-chart out the most titanic territorial imperative, we will go on a Journey. And the Journey, oh, do understand, oh, do feel, do see, will last a billion lifetimes" (Ray Bradbury, "Opening the Beautiful Door of True Immortality," *Los Angeles Times*, 20 November 1977, p. 50).

A Religious Experience

Bradbury gave a proper label to *Close Encounters* when he called it "a religious film." We should not take away any credit from the UFOs, for UFOs have created a mass experience in the seventies that accounts for a great deal of the film's appeal. But why are we so prone to preoccupation with the unknown and the future? Why is it that our minds yearn for tomorrow so desperately? Perhaps there are many reasons. Certainly, these are among them: fear of the unknown, loneliness, boredom, and a longing to soar beyond the limitations of this world and this time.

It is the faith and hope that people place in UFOs that is drawing them to see *Close Encounters*—in many cases time and time again. It is an optimistic faith that says things have *got* to get better! It is the hope of finding that greater identification with the universe, of learning what the future holds in store, of entering into a kind of immortality introduced in some utopian world of tomorrow by a mystical blend of advanced technology and speculative extraterrestrial intelligence.

Close Encounters is but one more gospel account in the new "bible" of today's space-age religion. It has its own theology, its own answers for the past, the present, and the future. It promises to open the door to immortality, and that is its major weakness. It asks us to place our faith in a transcendent technology. But, ironically, that is exactly what so many of us have already done, only to find it so unfulfilling, so frustratingly unsatisfactory.

Close Encounters can entertain like no movie before it has ever entertained, and UFOs can excite our imaginations like no phenomenon has ever excited us. Yet, neither *Close Encounters* nor UFOs can alleviate fear or hate, remove the guilt pent up within us, or really offer us the immortality that our souls cry out for so hopefully, so desperately.

Incredibly, though, there are millions of ordinary people walking the earth at this very moment who have found an answer to those problems, which *Close Encounters* cannot provide. As a result, their fears have been dispelled, their guilt removed, and their wrongdoings forgiven. For them, the promises which cannot be delivered by tomorrow's hoped-for transcendent technology and today's secular humanism already have become fulfilled in another way. They have experienced a spiritual rebirth into a new life that is everlasting.

Though *Close Encounters* is but entertainment, its message, fanciful as it is, is based upon a very real phenomenon—unidentified flying objects. It is important therefore that we try to understand this phenomenon, because it is from the UFO mass experience that *Close Encounters* has borrowed those tenets upon which it bases the precepts of its theology. And that theology, packaged in the spectacular trappings of a new space-age religion, has many implications which challenge our long-held beliefs about the origin of the universe, life, God, the Bible, and immortality.

2

Behind the Scenes Encounters

During location filming of *Close Encounters of the Third Kind* in Alabama, an ominous mood was cast over the production when mysterious, turbulent thunder clouds filled the skies. Their appearance was an uncanny occurrence, since they looked very much like the clouds, which were seen in the film, out of which the UFOs swooped down from the heavens. Were the clouds an omen of more things to come? It's hard to say if there was any connection, but more unusual things *did* begin to happen!

On one occasion several members of the production had a real, live close encounter with a UFO. It happened one night during location filming in Alabama. John Veitch, Columbia Pictures' vice president in charge of production, saw the UFO, along with Steven Spielberg and several others.

"I was up in my office," recalled Veitch, "and I heard some commotion, and I ran outside behind the hangar. Off in the distance we saw what appeared like a crazy configuration of blinking lights—yellow, green, blue. Steven and the others had been watching it for some time."

Veitch watched the UFO as it finally disappeared off into the distant clouds.

Because of these and many other extraordinary experiences during the filming of *Close Encounters*, some of the production people said they now felt closer to God, and that being a part of the production had been a life-changing experience.

The onslaught of unusual events tapered off during the postproduction phase. Then, *Close Encounters* was premiered in Los Angeles and New York. Now, it really started happening—all over the world!

Earthshaking sonic booms occurred off the eastern coast, sending a wave of speculation up and down the eastern seaboard that a UFO invasion was about to begin. The government was deluged with demands for an explanation, but the experts were baffled by the phenomenon, and the UFO scare went on unabated.

A Voice From Outer Space

In Great Britain, meanwhile, thousands of TV viewers were stunned when all regular programming was interrupted by a voice which claimed to be that of Asteron. "All your weapons of evil must be destroyed," said the throaty voice to the TV viewers in southern England. "You have only a short time to learn to live together in peace." Many believed it was the voice of an extraterrestrial being, speaking from a UFO somewhere in the earth's atmosphere. The authorities were never able to find the answer to the puzzling TV ultimatum.

Reports of close encounters with UFOs began flooding such places as the Harvard-Smithsonian Center for Astrophysics. According to James Cornell, the center's public-affairs officer, reports were coming in at the rate of several a day. Cornell could offer no explanation to the callers and, in turn, was accused of being part of some government cover-up conspiracy.

The public's concern about these strange occurrences grew and grew, until in late 1977, President Jimmy Carter called on the National Aeronautics and Space Administration (NASA) to reopen its investigations of UFOs. It was a front-page story for days.

"Are we going to be invaded by UFOs?" people were asking. But while some believe this to be true, there are others who feel the questions surrounding the nature and purpose of UFOs can be explained by natural, logical reasoning, even though such answers are not yet known. It has even been suggested that *Close Encounters* has created a form of mass hysteria over UFOs.

Certainly, the film's makers had no inkling of the enormous impact their film would have on the consciousness of people. They suspected the picture would do well and that it would add fuel to the fiery controversy over UFOs. But the film is having a religious impact too—one which first hit the production company and crew during the filming.

"It Makes You Stop and Think"

Columbia's John Veitch, who considers himself a "religious person," talked about the effect the film was having on his religious outlook. "I wondered," recalled the film executive, " 'what is the good Lord thinking about all of this?' It made me realize that here we are on one little planet with so many millions of people on it, and I wondered what is taking place in outer space. It makes you stop and think. There's more to life than what we normally expect or think about."

Veitch said there was a genuine need on his part and the others in the production for direction and guidance from some source beyond themselves.

25

"An undertaking like this had never been done before, and none of us are that bright or that smart that we certainly couldn't use some outside help, and also guidance. And, evidently, that was happening.

"It made us aware, it made us think," Veitch went on. "What is going on? How was this universe created? What are we trying to show? What are we trying to tell with the story? What is the Supreme Being doing? How far is He going to let us go?"

The Creators of Close Encounters

Those were questions that ran through the minds of not only Veitch, but all the others who were involved in the creation of *Close Encounters.*

Close Encounters was filmed under the leadership of a talented team of experienced artists with major successes to their credit. This extraordinary production team is characterized for the most part by a surprising youthfulness.

The film was written and directed by Steven Spielberg, at the age of twenty-nine, from his own original story idea. It was Spielberg's first film since directing *Jaws,* which was motion picture's all-time box-office champion, having earned more than $400 million. For his work on *Jaws,* he was named director of the year by the United Motion Picture Association and nominated as best director by the Directors Guild of America.

Spielberg is a good friend of George Lucas, who wrote and directed *Star Wars,* and a leader among the growing number of new Hollywood filmmakers. He ranks in the forefront of the screen's most successful directors. Known and respected as a young man of many creative talents, he has boundless energy and an ability to accomplish the seemingly impossible on film.

Yet, as recently as 1973, Spielberg was still editing his first motion picture for theatrical release, *The Sugarland Express,* which starred Goldie Hawn and William Atherton as a couple of small-time crooks on the lam. Later, it drew widespread praise. Noted reviewer Pauline Kael wrote in *New Yorker* magazine: "This is one of the most phenomenal directorial debut films in the history of movies."

Up until then, Spielberg's recognition had stemmed from outstanding achievements in television, particularly as director of *Duel,* a television movie about a mysterious truck that pursues a man (Dennis Weaver) in his car. Released in theaters abroad, it set new box-office records and won a number of the major European film-festival awards.

Spielberg was preparing to film *Jaws* and editing *Sugarland Express* when he wrote the first twenty-five pages of his script for *Close Encounters of the Third Kind.* His approach would be different from that taken by moviemakers for years, ever since Georges Melies fired a plywood rocket at a cardboard moon in the early era of silent films. Instead, Spielberg rooted his imagery in the awesome body of UFO data, which has been growing daily, ever since "mystery airships" were first sighted in the skies over Europe during the late nineteenth century.

Preparing for Close Encounters

Spielberg conceived *Close Encounters* as a highly entertaining film, and one that would make a significant statement on the theory of visitations from outer space. Like millions of others the world

27

over, he was fascinated and aroused by UFOs and the questions they provoked.

He outlined his ideas to producers Julia Phillips, thirty-three, and Michael Phillips, thirty-four, who were then involved in postproduction work on the *The Sting* and preparation of *Taxi Driver*.

"As he outlined it," recalled Julia Phillips, "it was even more than a story about UFOs and a government's cover-up of the whole UFO matter. I know it is Steven's feeling, and we share it, that there is something happening up there. And we should be told about it."

Julia and Michael Phillips's reaction to Spielberg's idea was instantaneous. They took it to Columbia Pictures, where it was met with equal enthusiasm.

Spielberg, by now totally involved in *Jaws*, devoted his evenings to writing the full screenplay for *Close Encounters*.

The subject of UFOs had always intrigued Spielberg. As a sixteen-year-old high-school boy in Phoenix, he had filmed a two-and-a-half-hour, eight-millimeter film titled *Firelight*, about scientists' investigating strange lights in the sky.

When he finished his work on *Jaws*, Spielberg turned his full attention to what was to become an even bigger challenge in unique filmmaking. His next several months were occupied in refining the screenplay for *Close Encounters*. He changed the script frequently on the set during the filming, which has become his way of seeking perfection.

"The Next Walt Disney"

Steven Spielberg's only choice for the job of visual-effects coordinator was thirty-five-year-old

Douglas Trumbull, whom he calls "the next Walt Disney."

The magic Douglas Trumbull brought to the motion-picture screen by his special photographic effects for Kubrick's *2001: A Space Odyssey* reached dimensions previously unapproached. Yet, the visual effects he now has created and supervised for *Close Encounters* are, in his words, "an extension" of that.

Aware that since *2001*, Trumbull himself had directed a space drama, *Silent Running*, and may have turned away from designing special photographic effects for others, Spielberg was hesitant to ask him to join the *Close Encounters* production team. After trying unsuccessfully to find another qualified creative talent for the task, he returned to Trumbull, his first choice. When Spielberg detailed the project, Trumbull immediately said he would do it.

"I've been interested for several years in doing a UFO film myself, and Steve's story struck a chord with me," he says. "The idea of creating UFOs with what we have at our disposal, and making them seem absolutely real—that was challenging and appealing."

Creating Film Magic

Trumbull and his company took over an entire 13,500-square-foot building, converting it into a complete movie studio to meet the demands of *Close Encounters*. Rooms were installed for developing, optical printing, and editing. Other rooms were used for elaborate filming "stages" with dolly tracks running horizontally and vertically. Also housed within the complex were electronically operated control booths, a wood shop, metal shop, paint shop, and a miniature set-construction shop.

There also were areas for maintaining the intricate cameras and lights and for carrying on never-ending experiments with the new processes, techniques, and equipment involved.

It was here that Trumbull and his company created the film magic for *Close Encounters*. Meanwhile, with the location filming completed, vital and unusually complete postproduction operations went into high gear.

Near Trumbull's facility, in a private, high-security apartment overlooking Marina del Rey, Spielberg set up shop for the critical editing of the thousands of feet of exposed negative. All normal furnishings were removed from the apartment, and it was transformed into a fully equipped film-editing department, with the most modern viewing, cutting, and splicing machines and rack upon rack of film reels.

Spielberg now had complete privacy and close security, and he was away from the constant interruptions that would have proved distracting in cutting rooms within a major studio. He then turned his attention to what he has called "the most creative part of filmmaking," putting his motion picture into its final form.

Spielberg was joined by film editor Michael Kahn and two assistant editors. Kahn's work on such motion pictures as *Return of a Man Called Horse* and *Buster and Billie* and his being an Emmy winner for the motion picture for television *Eleanor and Franklin* had established him as one of the most skilled in his craft. Spielberg calls him "the most creative and enthusiastic film editor I have ever worked with."

Spielberg's hideaway editing site enabled him, on a moment's notice, to join Trumbull in supervising the special photographic effects, or to reach producers Julia Phillips and Michael Phillips at the Columbia Pictures offices. There, he still would film necessary inserts. And there, important sound mixing, dubbing, looping, and other postproduction tasks were in progress.

Outer-Space Music

Also at Columbia's Burbank Studio, Academy Award winner John Williams was conducting the recording of his elaborate music score, utilizing a one-hundred-ten-piece orchestra. Spielberg had selected Williams as musical director because of his feeling for the type of outer-space music needed for the film, having recently completed the scoring of *Star Wars*. In January 1978, Williams received the Golden Globe award for composing the scores for both *Close Encounters of the Third Kind* and *Star Wars* and the Academy Award for *Close Encounters of the Third Kind*.

Vilmos Zsigmond was Spielberg's director of cinematography. He was winner of the Best Cinematography Award from the National Society of Film Critics for *The Long Goodbye*. William Fraker was the director of photography for additional American sequences. For the special Indian sequences the director of photography was Douglas Slocombe. Two other outstanding cinematographers, John Alonzo and Lazslo Kovacs, contributed their talents to special scenes.

In all, more than two hundred fifty men and women comprised the production team that made *Close Encounters of the Third Kind* and have made it possible for millions of people to come as near to a close encounter with a UFO as they ever will.

Part 2

*Encountering the
UFO Phenomenon*

3

We Are Not Alone!

Below the star-studded heavens pictured in magazine and newspaper ads for *Close Encounters of the Third Kind* is a deserted ribbon of highway that stretches straight ahead to a hilly ridge on the distant horizon. The white strips at the side of the pavement converge at a point in a gap in the far-away hills, behind which is radiating a brilliant glow, arching high into the night sky.

What is it that lies ahead?

Then our eyes catch a riveting statement in the movie's ad: "We are not alone!"

What is making that glow in the sky? Why don't we see anyone in the ad? Where is everyone? What is happening on the other side of that mountain?

Someone—or something—is making that glow. Could it be a UFO?

We know that the movie *Close Encounters of the Third Kind* is fiction, but what about UFOs? Are *they* real? Are UFOs piloted by beings from outer space? How scientific are the investigations of

UFOs? How reliable are the witnesses? Is there any firm evidence to prove that UFOs exist? Has there been—as some have charged—a government cover-up? Is there a link between UFOs and religion? Was God a UFOnaut?

To Believe or Not to Believe

A special public meeting had been called by the air force in order to respond to local citizens' demands for a government explanation of the UFOs that had been buzzing the city of Muncie for the past several nights. Roy Neary listened as an old farmer who had witnessed the UFOs with him added an incredible tag to his testimony.

"I saw Big Foot once," said the farmer. "It was up in the Sequoia National Park. The winter of nineteen fifty-one."

Roy grimaced and covered his face as he saw his hope for an explanation dissipate.

"It had a foot on him," continued the old farmer, "thirty-seven inches, heel to toe. Made a sound I would not want to hear twice in my life" (Steven Spielberg, *Close Encounters of the Third Kind* [New York: Dell Publishing Co., Inc., 1977], p. 129).

The TV cameramen covering the meeting sniggered, and Major Benchley's investigative-team members confidently felt they now held the upper hand.

The Credibility of Witnesses

Because of poor testimonies like that of the old farmer in *Close Encounters*, or suspected unreliability for any variety of reasons, the credibility of UFO "eyewitnesses" has long been the frontal attack of skeptics. But some reports are quite reliable. Consider this one: "It was shortly after dark, and ten or twelve men all watched it. It seemed to move toward us, then partially away, then return, then depart. It was bluish at first, then reddish, then luminous but not solid."

This happens to be quoted from one of two official reports filed by President Jimmy Carter in 1973, while he was governor of Georgia. According to his report, he saw the strange object in Leary, Georgia, in October 1969. He stated that he was waiting for an outdoor meeting to begin when the sharply outlined, self-illuminated object appeared in the sky.

"I don't laugh at people anymore when they say they have seen UFOs, because I've seen one myself," Carter was quoted as saying.

While Jimmy Carter is the most prominent world figure to have filed a UFO sighting report, he is hardly alone. Numerous other well-known Americans believe they have sighted UFOs, among them, John Gilligan, former governor of Ohio; former astronauts James McDivitt and L. Gordon Cooper; and scores of people from all walks of life, including scientists, airline pilots, astronomers, and government officials.

Not long ago, Senator Barry M. Goldwater, a major general in the air-force reserve, accepted a position on the board of governors of the prestigious National Investigation Committee on Aerial Phenomenon (NICAP).

Can So Many People Be Wrong?

The actual number of UFO sightings in America is a staggering fifteen million, according to a 1973 Gallup poll. This figure represents 11 percent of the country's adult population. Can so many people be wrong? Did they suffer from hallucinations? Did they simply misperceive natural occurrences such as weather balloons, satellites, planets, ball lightning, and the like? While many reported sightings could be explained away in this manner, scientists and other experts estimate that 20 to 30 percent are true unidentified flying objects—aerial phenomena that cannot be explained away.

Close Encounters of the Third Kind showed a scene from an air-traffic-control center located somewhere in Indiana, where a UFO was picked up on radar and tracked for several minutes. There are numerous reports of UFOs being tracked on radar, buzzing jumbo jets, and being fired upon by anti-aircraft missiles and jet fighters.

What are UFOs? Do they originate outside our solar system? Do they represent attempts by intelligent beings to observe or contact us?

Doctor J. Allen Hynek believes that solving the mystery of UFO phenomena will lead to a "quantum jump" in our scientific knowledge. But other experts disagree, such as aviation editor Phillip Klass, who believes there is a "prosaic, terrestrial" answer for every UFO sighting, however bizarre.

The Legend of the "Flying Saucers"

The motion picture, *Close Encounters*, more than anything else in recent times, is keeping the intriguing legend of the flying saucers alive.

Author Jacques Vallee, who holds degrees in mathematics and astronomy and is a consultant on NASA's "Mars Map" project, believes the legend of flying saucers is as old as man himself. In his book, *Anatomy of a Phenomenon: UFOs in Space,* Vallee tells how flying saucers got their name. He quotes a story from the January 25, 1878 edition of the *Denison Daily News* (Texas). It concerns a farmer, John Martin, who lived a few miles south of Denison. The story tells how Martin saw a dark flying object in the shape of a disk cruising high in the sky "at a wonderful speed," and used the word *saucer* to describe its shape (Jacques Vallee, *Anatomy of a Phenomenon: UFOs in Space* [New York: Ballantine Books, 1974], p. 1).

But it wasn't until some seventy years later that the name *flying saucers* caught on. It was the year 1947, and another man, Kenneth Arnold, spotted nine strange flying objects and called them "flying saucers." That name stuck for a while, but soon gave way to UFO for "unidentified flying object," because of so many reports of unidentified flying objects which were *not* shaped like saucers.

Flying the Friendly Skies—For Centuries

Close Encounters' mother spaceship was anything but new in appearance. Roy Neary thought it looked like an old oil refinery, with huge tanks and pipes and working lights everywhere. As he watched the phantom mass sliding across the canyon sky to the landing pad, it struck him how the ship seemed old and dirty—"junky"—like part of an old inner city or a giant old ship that had been sailing among the stars for thousands of years.

Could it be that UFOs have been cruising our atmosphere for centuries? Some experts believe this to be true and support their position on what they consider to be the evidence of history.

For many centuries, people have been recording observations of strange apparitions in the skies all over the world. It is estimated there were more than

39

ten thousand recorded sightings for all time, up to 1954 (Zola Levitt and John Weldon, *UFO's: What on Earth Is Happening?* [Irvine, CA: Harvest House, 1975], p. 20, note 2). UFOlogists get excited about these entries in the annals of history, because they believe that what these ancients saw and recorded are the same kinds of UFOs being observed today.

Their descriptions of these UFOs are understandably vividly colored by the cultures of the day. For example, an American Indian legend describes "baskets that come down from the sky." Among the Sioux Indians a legend says that the "sky people" returned to their home by turning themselves into arrows and taking flight into the heavens (J. Allen Hynek and Jacques Vallee, *The Edge of Reality: A Progress Report on Unidentified Flying Objects* [Chicago: Henry Regnery Company, 1975], p. 247).

Ancient Encounters?

While the legends of UFOs are common to many cultures throughout history and the world, the sightings of these strange objects have been interpreted in many ways—as the evil omens of demons and the "signs in the skies" of gods.

Another theory, and one which is quite popular among modern writers, is that the objects are the works of unknown civilizations, perhaps extraterrestrial beings. Such a theory, while supported by little fact, is not without grounds for speculation.

Granite carvings found in China, perhaps dating to 45,000 B.C., depict several beings with large torsos standing on cylindrical objects in the sky and below them, two others standing on the ground.

40

They were discovered in China's Hunan Mountain and on an island in Lake Tungting by Tschi Pen Lao of the University of Peking. Do these carvings represent ancient UFOnauts? Could they be based on some primitive myth or religious concept? Or, are they simply the works of fantasy by a Steven Spielberg of centuries ago?

In Europe, a vast collection of "UFO designs" has been discovered in some seventy-two caves scattered across France and Spain. These intriguing drawings are estimated to date from 13,000 B.C. Are they the records of ancients who witnessed a UFO invasion? Do they, like the cave sculptures of China, possibly have a mythological or religious significance. Or, are they, too, works of fantasy, the products of sheer imagination?

Stone sculptures in the Sahara, which have been estimated to date from 6,000 B.C., show humanlike beings with strange round heads. Some UFOlogists have suggested that these are likenesses of extraterrestrials who, having just stepped off their spaceship, are still wearing space helmets.

However, archaeology has discovered that the drawings and carvings and sculptures of the ancients oftentimes were more representative than realistic, which could indicate that the Sahara sculptures are representations of human beings that were made by either a surrealist artist, or else one with little artistic talent! Can you imagine what people centuries from now would think if they found a few representations of people by Picasso? Or what if they found some sketches of people drawn by a twentieth-century preschooler?—oversized heads, pear-shaped torsos, sticklike limbs, and no feet!

41

Perhaps some of the experts are forming conclusions more on supposition than on facts.

Write It Like It Is

The record of *written* history is a bit more precise than earlier artists' representations. In light of occasional written references, it is generally agreed by scholars and experts that people down through the centuries have been observing strange phenomenon such as our modern UFOs.

John Weldon, in his excellent book, *UFO's: What on Earth Is Happening?*, writes that a thousand years before Christ, Hindu writers told about "celestial and aerial cars," describing one of them as "a bright cloud in the sky." A blazing, spinning missile which radiates light and intense heat is referred to in the epic Hindu poem, "Mahabharata." And, highly maneuverable flying disks are mentioned in the "Samarangana."

Glowing flying objects, used by persons of special religious status, are referred to in some ancient Tibetan books (Weldon, *UFOs* p. 23).

Again, we must ask ourselves: What do these references mean? Are they based on myths or religion or fantasy, or could they be valid descriptions of bona fide UFOs?

A Pharaoh's Fantasy?

The Egyptians, who were scientifically advanced compared to other cultures of their era, also recorded sightings of strange objects in the sky. In what has been attributed to the annals of Pharaoh Thutmose III (circa 1504–1450 B.C.), there is a report of an encounter with "circles of fire" in the sky.

According to the Pharaoh's annals, the fire circles

were brighter than the sun, had a terrible stench about them (which is a common report about UFOs), were great in number, and appeared in the skies for a period spanning several days (Vallee, *Edge of Reality*, p. 4).

Pliny, Seneca, Tacitus, and many other reliable Roman historians in the centuries immediately before Christ, wrote about strange flying objects in the skies, calling them "fire balls," "fire shields," and "phantom ships."

For five centuries after the birth of Christ, recorded history is all but void of the mention of unidentified flying objects. Then, with the coming of the Middle Ages, apparent UFO activity resumed, or at least historians began recording sightings. They called these mystifying objects "cloudships" and "luminous strangers."

Gregory of Tours, the sixth-century French historian, wrote about "globes of fire" that traveled the skies. Then, from the eleventh to the seventeenth centuries, "wyld fire" fell from the skies, killing people and animals, at various times.

A scant four hours before Christopher Columbus sighted land on October 11, 1492, he saw a "glimmering light" from the deck of the *Santa Maria*. The object reportedly vanished, then reappeared several times (Weldon, *UFOs* p. 25, note 15).

To Believe or Not to Believe

One of the interesting characteristics of the UFOs depicted in *Close Encounters*, is their ability to appear as one object, then divide into several, only to reunite. Such a phenomenon (which is not uncommon among UFO reports) was mentioned centuries ago by none other than William Shakespeare. In his

King Henry VI (published about 1600), we find this interesting dialogue in part 3, act 2, scene 1:

> Edward: Dazzle mine eyes, or do I see three suns?
>
> Richard: Three glorious suns, each a perfect sun; Not separated with the racking clouds, But sever'd in a pale clear-shining sky. See, see! They join, embrace and seem to kiss, As if they vow'd some league inviolable: Now are they one lamp, one light, one sun, In this the heaven figures some event.

Were Shakespeare's "three glorious suns" which became a "perfect sun" fifteenth-century descriptions of UFOs? No other explanation has been proven.

Those Incredible Unidentified Contraptions

The machine age had arrived in America and, by the nineteenth century, people were being dazzled by the introduction of amazing new gadgets for industry, farm, and home. Consequently, UFOs were no longer reported as "fire balls" and "glorious suns," but, instead, as mechanical contraptions. Strange flying machines, not totally unlike those designed by Leonardo daVinci and fantasied by Jules Verne, began to appear in reports of sightings in the skies over major American cities, among them Chicago and San Francisco.

An engraving from a *San Francisco Call* edition in November 1896 depicted an airship kind of object, complete with propellers, a "passenger" compartment with portholes, and brilliant searchlights. It was quite a sensation at the time.

Perhaps the most bizarre UFO-related story concerned the alleged abduction of a cow from the farm of Alexander Hamilton near Le Roy, Kansas, in 1897. Awakened by noise in the corral, Hamilton summoned his son and a tenant to go with him to investigate. What they saw was a three-hundred-foot-long cigar-shaped object with an airship-type gondola slung underneath. Hamilton stated there were six strange beings inside. As the three men watched, Hamilton's cow was hoisted into the sky by a cable attached to the UFO. Moving westward, the UFO disappeared over the horizon.

The next day, Hamilton discovered that a neighboring farmer, Link Thomas, had found the remains of the cow on his property—hide, legs, and head. He identified the carcass as Hamilton's missing cow by the brand on the hide.

The story was never disproved, and no other explanation was ever offered for what had happened to Hamilton's cow.

Ghost Flyers

The early years of the twentieth century were marked by periods of numerous sightings of UFOs over brief periods of time. Called "flaps," these multiple sightings occurred across America in 1909 and 1918, and reports of sightings were received from other countries. These were war years, and because of scares about superior air weapons, people were beginning to ask if Germany had developed some amazing new type of dirigible. So vocal had the Americans become that Germany was prompted to officially deny any involvement with the UFO sightings.

By the 1930s, UFO sightings were reported from

around the world. Stories circulated about hot pursuits by aircraft. The Swedes had so many sightings they even had a name for the mysterious airships—"ghost flyers."

World War II brought on numerous reports of UFO sightings. Pilots of many nations filed reports, some of them speculating that the strange flying objects were secret air weapons of the enemy. Allied pilots called them "foo-fighters" and "Kraut-balls," names which were used in official postflight reports.

The Age of Flying Saucers

The "airship" configuration of UFOs reported about the turn of the century had become a thing of the past. Now, these incredible objects were described as mechanical and having the ability to outrun even the fastest fighter aircraft.

The age of flying saucers began on June 21, 1947. That was the day that private pilot Ken Arnold saw the formation of nine unidentified flying objects. He later described them to the press as moving "like saucers skipping across water." The press quickly picked up on Arnold's description of "flying saucers." More than 150 papers picked up the story, and the name *flying saucer* was here to stay.

The enormous publicity surrounding Arnold's reports of flying saucers created a UFO mania that has remained with us to this day. The number of reported sightings of flying saucers increased sharply. It isn't known if this is because the actual number of sightings increased or if people, given courage by the Arnold publicity, were less reluctant to speak out.

Within days after Arnold's reported encounter, several flying saucers were spotted at Maxwell Air

Force Base in Alabama, then seen over the White Sands Proving Grounds in New Mexico. Sightings were reported also at the Fairfield-Suisun Air Force Base in California and the Muroc Air Base (renamed Edwards Air Force Base).

Several months later, on January 7, 1948, air-national-guard pilot Thomas Mantell crashed after pursuing a UFO to twenty-thousand feet without an adequate oxygen supply. Only fifteen days later the air force officially launched Project Sign, the first of several flying-saucer-investigation programs that were to follow.

Take Us To Your President!

Jimmy Carter isn't the only president to have a close encounter with a UFO. In the summer of 1952, during the administration of Harry S Truman, the restricted air zone around the White House was violated by a swarm of UFOs. Air-force jets were scrambled immediately and gave chase. But the UFOs vanished from the scene at speeds up to seven thousand miles per hour, and disappeared from radar.

The unsuccessful jets returned to base. Minutes later, the UFOs reappeared, and once more the jets were scrambled. This time, as before, the case ended in failure. For the next several hours, the air-force jets and the UFOs played a kind of hide-and-seek game. Finally, the UFOs called the whole thing off and disappeared.

Something Is Out There

From the time the Romans began reporting "fire balls," to the "foo-fighters" seen by World War II pilots, and today's sightings of UFOs, it is clear that

47

thousands of people down through the ages have seen in the skies strange flying objects which could not be explained.

Today, we find reputable scientists taking up the matter of UFOs—some unswervingly maintaining that UFOs are real, and others just as adamantly denying that they are.

But one thing is certain: there is a large number of reported close encounters with UFOs by reliable people, which can neither be refuted nor be attributed to natural causes. For this reason, many people believe that UFOs are spacecraft piloted by extraterrestrial beings of superior intelligence, who are on the verge of making official contact with the governments of the planet earth. What if they are right?

Close Encounters of the Third Kind shows us "what if . . . ." The film speculates—no, predicts—what it would be like at that moment in the not-too-distant future when two kinds of intelligent beings reach out across the vastness of the universe and make contact.

4

The Cosmic Cover-up

In *Close Encounters of the Third Kind,* the air force's Major Benchley and his team of UFO investigators are clearly depicted in a debunking operation. Roy Neary and several others who had had close encounters with UFOs attended a special meeting reluctantly called by the government in order to answer local citizens' demands for an official answer to the UFO phenomenon.

Major Benchley, in an obvious gesture to embarrass the citizens in front of the well-represented news media, started off the meeting by holding up a large color photo of an eerie, high-revolution disk in blurred flight.

The group broke in spontaneous oohs and ahs, followed by confirming comments that the photo was indeed a UFO—like ones some of them had seen!

Then Major Benchley explained that the photo was really that of a pewter saucer thrown across the yard by one of his kids. Needless to say, the crowd knew it wouldn't get any straight answers from Major Benchley or any of his team. Clearly, the meeting was an attempt to discredit the "eyewitnesses" and to discourage them from pressing the matter further.

Deception at Devil's Tower

As the movie approached its highly charged climax, Roy and Jillian are found being guided by some mysterious force to a mammoth Wyoming rock pile called Devil's Tower, where they hope to find Jillian's abducted little boy, Barry, and discover why Roy has been so obsessed with the image of Devil's Tower.

They arrive, independently, in Wyoming, only to find there is a mass exodus of people who are attempting to escape from the deadly fumes of G-M nerve gas, accidently released as the result of a train derailment, so the U. S. Army would have the public believe.

Because Roy and Jillian—and a few others who were mysteriously drawn there—refuse to leave, they are interrogated by the army and then scheduled for evacuation by helicopter. They suspect the government has staged the disaster as a cover-up for some sort of covert operation being conducted in the vicinity, and manage to escape in order to seek out for themselves the intriguing secret of Devil's Tower.

Cover-Up Charged

The movie's theme of a government cover-up of UFO activity is based upon the conviction of a number of experts that in real life the United States government has engaged in a UFO cover-up for the past three decades.

One of those experts is Dr. J. Allen Hynek, who was Steven Spielberg's technical guide on UFO-logy in the making of the film. Hynek, former director of Ohio State University's McMillin Observatory and now on the faculty of Northwestern University, became the nation's leading UFO sleuth in 1948 when he was retained by the air force to head Project Blue Book, a continuing study of UFO phenomena.

Doctor Hynek admits he was skeptical when he began the project, but then became a "convert." After more than twenty years of investigation into some 12,600 reported UFO sightings, he estimates that 95 percent of them were of IFOs—*identified* flying objects such as planes, the planet Venus, or weather balloons. But the remaining 5 percent remain unexplained.

He is disturbed by what he considers the official attempt to dismiss UFO sightings as hoaxes and hallucinations.

"How can hallucinations appear on radar, break tree branches, and scare animals?" he asked. "How can they leave physical traces or stop cars? We're dealing with something far more complex than hallucinations or apparitions."

Doctor Hynek's speculation contradicted the official air-force position that "no sightings, categorized as unidentified, represent technological developments beyond the range of present knowledge."

The breaking point for Dr. Hynek came in March 1966, when he took part in a Detroit press conference during which the air force explained a baffling display of lights over Michigan as the result of "swamp gas."

Only a few weeks later, Dr. Hynek told a congressional committee that the air-force findings were, in his opinion, prejudiced and inadequate.

"To put it bluntly," he told an interviewer some years later, "the air force was under orders from the Pentagon to debunk UFOs."

Doctor Hynek left his consulting position with the air force and founded the Center for UFO Studies in Evanston, Illinois. The center carries on the monumental task of computerizing, cataloging,

51

and investigating more than 100 daily reports of UFO sightings. It was here that Steven Spielberg sought the information upon which to base *Close Encounters of the Third Kind*. He even found the film's title in one of Dr. Hynek's books, *The UFO Experience*.

In his book, Dr. Hynek had categorized UFO sightings into three kinds of "close encounters." The first kind involved sighting a UFO. The second involved some physical evidence of the encounter. And, a "close encounter of the third kind" was one in which actual contact was made with the occupants of a UFO.

Project Sign

It was a close encounter of the first kind in 1947 by Kenneth Arnold that launched the modern era of American flying-saucer sightings. His widely publicized sighting was the beginning of many UFO reports to be received by the government. For the next two years, these UFO reports were referred to the Air Technical Intelligence Center (ATIC) at Wright-Patterson Air Force Base in Dayton, Ohio, the agency responsible for analyzing intelligence information for the air force.

Two opinions emerged about UFOs. One took the position that UFOs are probably interplanetary and that the military should be placed on alert. The other position dismissed all reports of UFO sightings as misperceptions or hallucinations or some other rational cause.

But the reports of UFO sightings continued to pile up at ATIC at Wright-Patterson. Finally, in February 1948, the government set up a separate and formal project, called Project Sign, to evaluate the UFO situation. Project Sign never quite lived to be a year old. It was replaced by Project Grudge which debunked the reports of UFO encounters. But it, too, had a short life; the air force announced on December 27, 1949, that Project Grudge had completed its mission to evaluate UFO reports, and therefore was terminated.

UFO reports were received after that at ATIC, but evidently little, if any, investigation was conducted.

In March 1952, Project Blue Book was formed under the leadership of Captain E. J. Ruppelt to investigate UFO reports. Then, in July of that year, a major UFO flap occurred in the nation's capital. Captain Ruppelt described the historic and now famous incident in his book, *Report on Unidentified Flying Objects* (New York: Doubleday & Company, 1956):

When radars at the Washington National Airport and at Andrews AFB, both close to the nation's capital, picked up UFOs, the sightings beat the Democratic National Convention out of headline space. They created such a furor that I had inquiries from the office of the President of the United States and from the press in London, Ottawa, and Mexico City. A junior-sized riot was only narrowly averted in the lobby of the Roger Smith Hotel in Washington when I refused to tell the U.S. newspaper reporters what I knew about the sightings.

Besides being the most highly publicized UFO sightings in the Air Force annals, they were also the most monumentally fouled-up messes that repose in the files.

53

Enter the CIA

While the air force was concerned about the heavy volume of reports coming in following the "Washington Flap" of 1952, the CIA got interested in UFOs. The CIA thought that enemy agents might clog military communications with a barrage of false flying-saucer reports to serve as a smoke screen for a sneak attack on the country.

Subsequently, on December 4, 1952, the Intelligence Advisory Committee recommended that the CIA convene a special investigative panel of selected scientists to look into the mounting number of UFO reports. This panel was to become known as the "Robertson Panel," so named after its chairman, Dr. H. P. Robertson, a noted physicist and relativity expert.

According to Dr. Hynek, the Robertson Panel's report set Project Blue Book on the road to debunking UFO reports. He quoted part of the panel's report: "The Panel further concludes . . . that the continued emphasis on the reporting of these phenomena does, in these parlous times, result in a threat to the orderly functioning of the protective organs of the body politic . . . . We cite as examples the clogging of channels, the danger of being led by continued false alarms to ignore real indications of hostile actions, and the cultivation of a morbid national psychology in which skillful hostile propaganda could induce hysterical behavior and harmful distrust of duly constituted authority" (J. Allen Hynek, *The Hynek UFO Report* [New York: Dell Publishing Co., Inc. 1977], p. 22).

The government went to great lengths to dampen public interest in UFOs. Doctor Hynek, who was an associate member of the Robertson Panel, recalls one suggestion that Walt Disney produce a cartoon in which Mickey Mouse would ridicule UFOs. However, there is no record of such a film having ever been produced.

Then reports appeared in the press that the Robertson Panel was being financed and controlled by the CIA. This only added to the public's growing fascination with UFOs. People were beginning to ask what the government was trying to hide.

The Condon Report

In 1966, the air force contracted with the University of Colorado to conduct an extensive study of UFO phenomena. The project was headed by physicist Edward U. Condon.

The University of Colorado report (the "Condon Report"), based on the results of the study, titled *Scientific Study of Unidentified Flying Objects*, reached the following conclusions: (1) there was no evidence that the subject of UFOs had been "shrouded in official security"; (2) UFOs did not constitute any hazard to national security; (3) two decades of UFO study had made no significant contribution to scientific knowledge; and (4) further extensive study of the general topic could not be expected to contribute meaningfully to the advancement of science.

The study was reviewed by a panel of the National Academy of Sciences, which agreed with the conclusions of the Condon Committee and further commented: "On the basis of present knowledge the least likely explanation of UFOs is the hypothesis of extraterrestrial visitations by intelligent beings."

Finally, in 1969, the government closed the book

on Project Blue Book and some twenty-two years of expensive investigation into UFOs.

NASA Says No to the President

Since the U.S. government discontinued Project Blue Book, reported sightings of UFOs have kept coming in to NASA. Without funds and personnel to properly study the reports, they simply pile up, unnoticed!

This has caused many UFO-research proponents to call on the government to reopen its UFO investigations—so much so, in fact, that Jimmy Carter made it a campaign promise.

Then, a space phenomenon of another kind exploded upon the American public in the summer of 1977—George Lucas's science-fantasy movie, *Star Wars*.

Lucas's film excited people like no film before it ever had. Critics predicted it would become the all-time top-grossing motion picture in history and the box-office receipts seemed to confirm it.

Perhaps it was *Star Wars* which motivated people during the summer of 1977 to deluge the White House with letters and telegrams urging President Carter to reopen the government's investigation of UFOs.

The president responded favorably by requesting that NASA consider taking up the study where Project Blue Book had left off in 1969. The actual request was in the form of a letter in July 1977 from the president's science advisor, Dr. Frank Press, to NASA administrator Robert A. Frosch. Frosch then passed on the request to his assistant for special projects, Dave Williamson, for evaluation and advisement.

Williamson and a team of technical advisors spent the next several months considering the merits of reopening the UFO investigations, then gave their recommendation—which was negative—to Frosch, in late December. The NASA administrator then informed Dr. Press by letter that such a study would be "wasteful and probably unproductive." But, Frosch added, NASA stood ready to analyze any "bona fide physical evidence from credible sources"—evidence which has never before been introduced.

It is interesting that evidence of a *non*physical nature evidently would not be analyzed by NASA, particularly since a widely held theory among many experts today is that UFOs might not be physical at all. This theory will be discussed in more detail in the next chapter.

NASA's rejection of the president's request was accepted by Dr. Press, who told the news media that he had no plan to pursue the matter further. The president's reaction, however, was never made public!

The Official Position

NASA's official position on UFOs remains unchanged from the time it was publicly announced in July 1976: "NASA is not involved in research concerning unidentified flying objects. Reports of unidentified objects entering U.S. air space are of interest to the U.S. military as a regular part of defense surveillance, but no government agency is conducting an ongoing investigation of UFOs at this time."

While NASA has closed the door on UFO investigations, the agency's interest in the subject of the possibility of life in outer space has led to its conducting a symposium on extraterrestrial intelligence (ETI) February 24, 25, 1977, at Ames Research Center in Mountain View, California.

NASA is not the only agency of the U.S. government that has addressed the UFO phenomenon. Cadets of the U.S. Air Force Academy at Colorado Springs were once taught: "The most stimulating theory for us is that the UFOs are material objects which are either 'manned' or remote-controlled by beings who are alien to this planet. There is some evidence supporting this viewpoint" (quoted from "Unidentified Flying Objects," *Introductory Space Systems,* vol. 2 [Colorado Springs: U.S. Air Force Academy]).

In direct contradiction, this statement is made in the Condon Report: "No direct evidence whatever of a convincing nature now exists for the claim that any UFOs represent spacecraft visiting Earth from another civilization . . . ."

If our government is being honest with us that there is *no* evidence to support the outer-space origin of UFOs, then why were air-force cadets taught that there *is* evidence to support such a theory? And why was the president's request denied?

Is there a cosmic cover-up in our government? Or is the inconsistency in dealing with the UFO issue only one more example of bureaucracy's right hand not knowing what its left hand is doing?

5

Encountering UFOs

The UFO phenomenon has posed a mystery to man perhaps from the time of his earliest existence. UFOs have evoked strong emotions and great curiosity among the people of many nations and cultures.

Close Encounters of the Third Kind showed people responding to UFOs with awe and near reverence over the strange and wonderful mystery they saw being answered after so many centuries of waiting and speculating.

Columbia Pictures' John Veitch expressed it this way: "I think [*Close Encounters*] pointed out that this alien force or this alien phenomenon, whatever it is, is not dangerous. Let's not in our own minds have everybody being the enemy. Let's be just; let's be fair. Let's present what we think is happening and what will happen. And, if there is eventually a landing of a spaceship, let's be able to extend to them love and fellowship . . . . Let's not assume that we have to go out there with cannons and guns and be ready to kill them."

But curiously omitted from *Close Encounters* were the *negative* aspects of the nature of UFOs. If official UFO reports showed that these beings behaved in a benevolent way, then we could see justification for the philosophical view of UFOs taken by the film's producers. But the records show that many people have experienced emotional and physical trauma as a result of fear and anxiety stemming from their close encounters. According to these reports, UFOs have been responsible for abductions (like Barry Guiler), murder, rape, and property damage, to list but a few not-so-nice activities they are said to carry on.

Fear of Mass Hysteria

Ordinary citizens are not alone among those interested in UFOs.

The military has been interested in UFOs because of their possible threat to national security and because of their potential to create mass hysteria and riots of such magnitude that communications, transportation, and other critical needs of society could be thrown into a topsy-turvy state of confusion, if not total inoperation.

The science community also has expressed keen interest in UFOs. It is thought among many scientists that UFOs might give clues about the origin of the universe, the existence of other life forms in outer space, and the very source of life and creation.

But What Are UFOs?

The federal government, with more than thirty years of intensive research into reported UFO encounters of various kinds, has been unable to adequately answer the question, "What are UFOs?" A typical answer is this one, offered by the U.S. Air Force, which states that a UFO is "any aerial phenomenon or object which is unknown or appears to be out of the ordinary to the observer" (U.S. Air Force Regulation 80–17, September 19, 1966).

That's a pretty broad definition! It could include any number of natural objects or phenomena which, when not recognized by the observer, remain unknown and mysterious.

As stated earlier, Dr. J. Allen Hynek, who has spent more than twenty years investigating some 12,600 reported UFO sightings, estimates that as many as 95 percent of them were IFOs—*identified* flying objects! Only the remaining 5 percent, says Dr. Hynek, are truly unidentified.

"They're Following Us!"

When I was ten years old, I could have been one of those statistics, because I had a "close encounter." It happened one crisp fall night in 1950. The full moon was so bright that my Dad hardly needed the car's headlights on to see the highway ahead. Our family was driving from our ranch, located north of Pikes Peak in the central Colorado Rockies, to a PTA meeting at our school in the little mountain town of Woodland Park, some five miles away.

Suddenly, my younger brother, Dan, shouted out, "Look! What's that?"

We all glanced out to the right of the car. Immediately, we saw "them" too—four or five bluish white, luminous objects, flying low in formation, almost parallel to our car. They were narrow oblongs in shape (the "cigar-shaped" variety).

"They're flying saucers!" I said excitedly, hardly believing my own eyes.

The UFOs made no sound. They simply followed our car from a safe distance. How fascinating it was to watch them. They seemed almost playful, soaring gently upward, then rushing back down—sometimes toward us, and other times away.

Dad tried to outrace them. He stepped on the accelerator, but the flying saucers kept up right with us. Then, Dad slowed down to a snail's pace—and our friendly followers slowed down, too!

"Stop the car, Dad," I blurted out. He pulled over to the side of the road and braked the car to a halt. Dad got the flashlight from the glove compartment, then got out of the car. Dan and I followed him.

There, in a pasture, maybe a half mile away, we estimated, rested the flying saucers. We couldn't tell if they had landed or if they were suspended in the air. The flashlight obviously couldn't cast its beam that far, so we just stood there for a few minutes, watching in wonder.

After a while, we went back to the car and drove off. We looked out the right of the car and sure enough, the flying saucers were trailing us some distance off to the side. A mile or two farther down the road the flying saucers disappeared behind a hill, and we never saw them again.

Seeking an Explanation

For several days our family talked about the flying saucers, trying to come up with some explanation for them. Where had they come from, and what were they doing? I couldn't help but hope that someday I would see them again and maybe find out more about them.

One afternoon, not too many days later, as I rode home on the school bus, I noticed telephone crews stringing shiny new copper wires on poles along the roadside. The wires glistened brilliantly where the sun reflected off them. *Hey! I've seen that before!* I thought. Then it came together in my mind—the flying saucers! They had acted the same way as the sun's reflections on the telephone wires!

My family hadn't seen flying saucers at all, only the reflection of the bright full moon on the shiny copper telephone wires, down the road a mile or so.

I was disappointed. Somehow I had hoped I had seen real flying saucers and that maybe I'd see them again. Though we didn't report the incident to the authorities, this "close encounter" was like so many that are reported: it had a natural, logical explanation. What my family had seen were not UFOs, but IFOs, identified flying objects.

Unexplained Encounters

While the majority of reported UFOs are in reality IFOs, it is those which remain unexplained that intrigue so many people.

Doctor Hynek said in an interview, "Whatever one may think about UFOs—whatever one may believe about their physical reality—whatever one may speculate about their origins, one fact has stood out over the past quarter of a century: UFOs continue to be reported by people the world over, and in all walks of life.

"The contents of these reports continue to intrigue, mystify, entrance, and engage our imaginations," the scientist continued. "Even the skeptic can barely fail to sense the dramatic element in a well-documented, multiple-witnessed report of a UFO close encounter."

Hynek, who is one of the world's foremost astronomers and astrophysicists, admits that at first he was not a "believer."

His initial doubts began to disappear when he learned the phenomenon was global, not limited to the United States. The fact that reports from distant countries were almost identical to those in America, as to what they described, and the reputable sources of many reports—coming from airline pilots, trained radar operators, law officers, ministers, doctors, and apparently reliable citizens, even from air and military bases—led to his growing conviction.

Classifying the Unexplainable

Several years ago, Dr. Hynek devised a UFO classification system, based solely on what was reported as actually observed (and not the observer's opinion on the nature of the UFO encountered). Observation of unidentified lights in the evening skies are the most frequent type of report. Hynek called these *Nocturnal Lights*. The majority of daytime sightings, which could be the same objects seen as Nocturnal Lights, are usually reported as objects having an oval shape and metalliclike appearance. These are called *Daylight Disks* by Hynek.

Some UFOs are "observed" via radar. Of these, some are corroborated by visual sightings. Still other UFOs are seen visually, but are not detected on radar!

These three categories are helpful for classifying reports of UFOs seen from far distances. But for classifying reports of closer sightings, Dr. Hynek created a broad category called the *Close Encounters*. There are basically three kinds of close encounters.

Close Encounters of the First Kind (CE 1): Included in this classification are reported UFO sightings from a very close range, usually within a few hundred feet, or at least near enough for detail to be discerned.

Close Encounters of the Second Kind (CE 2): This grouping consists of UFO sightings followed by the finding of physical evidence, such as landing marks on the ground, scorched earth, or broken vegetation. Strangely, no "piece" of a UFO has, to this day, been authenticated. Still, some eight hundred cases of physical traces of UFO encounters have been cataloged by Ted Phillips (Hynek, *Hynek UFO Report*, p. 30; Phillips's catalog is available from the Center for UFO Studies, 924 Chicago Avenue, Evanston, IL 60202).

Close Encounters of the Third Kind (*CE 3*): Steven Spielberg borrowed the title of this category for his hit film. This kind of encounter is, obviously, the most dramatic of the reported UFO sightings. These reported encounters include those in which occupants of UFOs, or UFOnauts, are seen and, in some cases, physical contact is made with them. A listing of more than a thousand reported close encounters of the third kind has been compiled (ibid. p. 31).

Describing the Unexplainable

UFO reports can contain scant descriptive information or they can be greatly detailed. A number of cataloging systems have been devised, and they have some common factors. A textbook formerly used by the Air Force Academy uses the following outline:

Appearance
  a. Size
  b. Shape (disk, ellipse, football, and so on)
  c. Luminosity
  d. Color
  e. Number of UFOs
Behavior
  a. Location (altitude, direction, and so on)

   b. Patterns of paths (straight line, climbing, zigzagging, and so on)

   c. Flight characteristics (wobbling, fluttering, and so on)

   d. Periodicity of sightings

   e. Time duration

   f. Curiosity or inquisitiveness

   g. Avoidance

   h. Hostility

Associated Effects

   a. Electromagnetic (compass, radio, ignition systems, and so on)

   b. Radiation (burns, induced radioactivity, and so on)

   c. Ground disturbance (dust stirred up, leaves moved, standing wave peaks on surface of water, and so on)

   d. Sound (none, hissing, humming, roaring, thunderclaps, and so on)

   e. Vibration (weak, strong, slow, fast)

   f. Smell (ozone or other odor)

   g. Flame (how much, where, when, color)

   h. Smoke or cloud (amount, color, persistence)

   i. Debris (type, amount, color, persistence)

   j. Inhibition of voluntary motion by observers

   k. Sighting of "creatures" or "beings"

After Effects

   a. Burned areas or animals

   b. Depressed or flattened areas

   c. Dead or missing animals

   d. Mentally disturbed people

   e. Missing items

("Unidentified Flying Objects," *Introductory Space Systems*, vol. 2, [Colorado Springs: U.S. Air Force Academy])

Space here will not allow any attempt to present available data on these descriptions; however, there are numerous books available which contain hundreds of case histories.

UFO Theories

As extensive as UFO studies have been over the past three decades, science has been unable to advance any explanation for the nature and origin of UFOs beyond the theory stage. There are only a few theories that have been advanced to date. They can be grouped as follows: natural phenomena; hallucinations, hoaxes, and lunatics' ravings; secret weapons; alien beings; and spiritual.

Natural phenomena. As previously discussed, experts estimate that up to 95 percent of UFO reports can be attributed to misperceptions of natural objects and phenomena. These estimates are based on actual investigation into UFO reports in which identifiable causes have been uncovered. Some of these conclusively proved to be weather balloons and skyhook balloons, the planet Venus, man-made satellites, conventional aircraft, unusual cloud formations, and lights from ceilometers (equipment which projects light beams on cloud bases to determine the height of the aircraft visual ceiling).

Investigators also suspected that people have reported mirages, optical illusions, swamp gas, and ball lightning. You have never heard of ball lightning? Well, it is a little-understood discharge of electrical energy which forms a ball shape no bigger than an orange, which may last up to fifteen minutes.

Hallucinations, hoaxes, and lunatics' ravings. The "mystery airships" that were first "sighted" in the skies over Europe during the late nineteenth century were at first dismissed as hallucinatory hysteria. Indeed, some people believe today that UFO flaps or mass reports of UFO sightings confirm the "mass hysteria" or "hallucination" theory. Without doubt, a number of UFO reports can be attributed to hallucinations, hoaxes, and lunatics' ravings. But medical examinations of some reliable eyewitnesses (oftentimes pilots and military observers) fail to conclude the reported UFO sightings as unauthentic.

Secret weapons. This theory has pretty well run its course. Still, there are many Americans who insist that UFOs are secret weapons of the Russians. But, then, some Russians insist that UFOs are secret weapons of the Americans!

Alien beings. This is the theory popularized by most science-fiction movies and books. It is out of the public's fascination with speculation of contact with alien beings that *Close Encounters of the Third Kind* owes much of its success. And now the movie is proving to be a major influence in promoting the alien-being theory to a growing new multitude of UFO "converts."

Spiritual. This theory holds that since science has been unsuccessful in solving the UFO riddle through scientific analysis of natural phenomenon, UFOs then must have a supernatural or spiritual nature. This theory further divides into two subtheories: first, that these UFOs are empowered by a morally neutral force—that is, neither intrinsically good nor evil—and, second, that UFOs are probably occult, or demonic in nature.

The first two theories mentioned above—natural phenomenon and emotional causes—contribute to explaining a large number of reported UFO encounters. The secret-weapons theory hardly merits consideration. But the remaining theories—alien beings and spiritual—deserve closer scrutiny because of their widespread acceptance and potential implications.

6

Are UFOs From Outer Space?

It is becoming more and more difficult to see the stars in heaven from within our inner cities these days because of air pollution and the competing glare of city lights. However, if you are fortunate to get away from the city—into the countryside, out in the desert, up in the mountains, or at the beach— then maybe there the air is clear enough and the surroundings dark enough for you to gaze in endless wonder at the depths of space.

Your first impulse is to locate the big dipper, then the little one. And maybe you can even spot one or more of the constellations. You try to comprehend the vast distances between yourself and the stars above. It's mind boggling.

Space: The Unknown Quantity

Our generation has placed men on the moon and sent probes to distant planets, to the sun, and beyond our own solar system. But what have we really *learned* about space? What do we know about it? Where does the universe end? (Don't all things have an end? But, then, what would be beyond the boundaries of the universe?) How did the universe get here? What caused it to happen?

Star gazing makes us get right down to the very basics of life: How did we get here? Where did life come from? What happens to our souls when we die? Does life simply get snuffed out like a candle? Or does the soul live on in some other dimension?

If you allow your thoughts to wander, you ask

71

yourself whether you believe there is life on other planets. Is there intelligent life? Is it *more* intelligent than ourselves? Are "they" trying to make contact with us earthlings? Will they help us or harm us?

Super Intelligence

The reasoning is that if surveying our planet from UFOs, there are extraterrestrial beings with such super intelligence that enables them to navigate among the planets and stars to reach our tiny planet, then surely they are smart enough to have outlawed crime and war. That line of reasoning sees the possibility that these extraterrestrials have become masters over those things which cause death and that they hold the key to the mysteries of immortality. And, maybe, they intend to teach *us* the secret way to obtain eternal life.

The advertisements for *Close Encounters of the Third Kind* boldly announce, "We are not alone!" It is surprising how many scientists share this speculation. They join Spielberg and company in the belief that we earthlings are not the only life forms in the universe. Basing their opinions largely on mathematical probability, they reason that, since there are billions of suns in the universe, apparently capable of supporting planetary systems, it would be miraculous if we didn't share the cosmos with other life forms.

Doctor Carl Sagan, the eminent astronomer, expresses his belief this way: "I think there can be an enormous number of civilizations in our galaxy alone. I calculate roughly one million civilizations among the planets of the Milky Way, most of them more technologically advanced than ours."

In *The UFO Experience*, anthropologist Margaret Mead pointed to our own space explorations to support her endorsement of the alien-being theory: "We're sending them [spacecraft] out. Why shouldn't someone be sending them here? Just think when Pioneer Ten leaves our solar system, *it* will become a UFO in other star systems."

Hello, Out There!

Doctor Mead notes the message from President Carter which was placed aboard Voyager II prior to its launching on August 20, 1977, to show that the president and our government evidently share the belief in alien beings. The president's message reads:

> We cast this message into the cosmos . . . of the two hundred billion stars in the Milky Way galaxy, some—perhaps many—may have inhabited planets and space-faring civilizations. If one such civilization intercepts Voyager and can understand these recorded contents, here is our message:
>
> "This is a present from a small distant world, a token of our sounds, our science, our images, our music, our thoughts, and our feelings . . . . This record represents our hope and our determination, and our good will, in a vast and awesome universe."

Strange Behavior

If UFOs are mechanical devices from outer space, they certainly don't behave according to the physical laws that govern mechanical things with which we are familiar. Some reports indicated that UFOs have the capacity to "materialize" or disappear with ease, sometimes under detection by radar and cameras, and other times not. The tremendous Mach-plus speeds at which UFOs reportedly travel should produce sonic booms as the sound barrier is broken, but UFO reports are strangely void of such occurrences.

Granted, reports of unidentified sonic booms off the east coast of the United States began to appear in newspapers in January 1978. But this is a periodic phenomenon, according to local sources, who say no explanation has ever been found. *Newsweek* magazine, in reporting the latest booms, indirectly questioned if the cause could be UFO related. So far, however, no evidence has turned up to indicate that this association is anything more than journalistic sensationalism, inspired no doubt by the tremendous popularity of *Close Encounters of the Third Kind.*

UFOs, if they were constructed of familiar metals and other materials, by traveling at great speeds through the earth's atmosphere, would create so much friction that they would burn up. Yet, the record carries no reports of disintegrating UFOs.

Equally strange is the reported maneuverability of UFOs. They are said to make superfast accelerations and stops, and even execute instant direction changes. No known material (or passengers) could withstand such physical stress.

One explanation offered for the physical-law-defying behavior of UFOs is that they might be operating under a *different* set of physical laws. But, unfortunately, such an argument has never been scientifically supported with evidence. On the contrary, our country's experiments in space indicate that the physical laws which govern earthbound people appear to be universal in nature.

Another question posed by many reports is, how can material UFOs change shape and color, and even "split"—like Shakespeare's "glorious sun"—into several objects, only to rejoin into a single unit again?

These are only some of the critical questions that remain unanswered by UFOlogists—questions which frankly embarrass many members of the scientific community.

The Transportation Problem

Doctor J. Allen Hynek admits there is difficulty in accepting the concept of cosmic travel: "As an astronomer, I know what distances are involved, and I don't think people appreciate how vast the universe is. For an alien civilization from another solar system to reach us, it would require technological skills so advanced that our science cannot envision them.

"Yet it is conceivable," he allowed. "Physicist Stanley Friedman has pointed out that to a man crossing the plains in a covered wagon one hundred years ago, the only imaginable way of bridging the distance between, say St. Louis and San Francisco, was by using faster horses. He couldn't begin to imagine a 747 jumbo jet.

"Perhaps, in our provincial way, we cannot conceive of what a truly advanced civilization might accomplish," Dr. Hynek concluded.

If alien beings have been buzzing the earth for centuries, what are they doing? What are they waiting for? Why haven't they made contact? Why hasn't a piece of material from a UFO ever been authenticated? Though UFOs have been fired upon by pilots of many nations, why hasn't a single one been captured or shot down? Why hasn't there been at least one radar report of a UFO entering earth's atmosphere?

What Are the Chances?

More basic than those questions is the one regarding the possibility of life itself in outer space. The theory of evolution is applied to show that if certain chemicals and other conditions are present, there could be all that is necessary for life to originate in outer space, then evolve into intelligent beings which pilot the UFOs which are cruising our skies. Is the existence of alien life by *chance* in outer space a possibility or an impossibility? This question is superbly dealt with in *UFOs: What on Earth Is Happening?*, by John Weldon and Zola Levitt:

In the October 1969 issue of *Nature* magazine, Dr. Frank Salisbury of Utah State University, currently on leave at the Division of Biomedical and Environment Research at the U.S. Atomic Energy Commission, examined the chance of one of the most basic chemical reactions for the continuation of life taking place. This reaction involves the formation of a specific DNA molecule. It is important to realize that Dr. Salisbury was assuming that life *already* existed. His calculations do not refer to the chance of the *origin* of life from dead matter—something infinitely more improbable—but to the continuance of life already existing.

He calculated the chance of this molecule

76

evolving on 10^{20} hospitable planets, or one hundred, thousand, million, billion planets. This is a figure with twenty zeros after it, and is at least one thousand times more hospitable planets than the number many scientists have estimated could exist. Dr. Salisbury allows four billion years for the chance coming into existence of this molecule on all these planets. But remember he is not speaking here of life as we know it—developed, intelligent living beings, or even of *one* single cell for that matter. He is only calculating the chance of this one appropriate DNA molecule.

He concluded that the chances of just this one tiny DNA molecule coming into existence over four billion years, with conditions just right, on just one of these almost infinite number of hospitable planets, including the earth, as *one chance* in 10^{415}. This is a number with 415 zeros after it. Such a large number is unimaginable . . . .

Even if we packed the entire universe with hospitable planets, so no place was left between them, the chance of this molecule forming on all these planets would still be *one* chance in a figure with 377 zeros after it (10^{58} planets would pack the universe with earth-size planets). This shows that life simply could not originate in outer space—period. But, you ask, isn't there still *one* chance in a number this size, even if it is so large? Given enough time, wouldn't eventually *anything* happen?

Dr. Emile Borel, one of the world's great experts on mathematical probability, formulated a basic law of probability. It states that the occurrence of any event where the chances are beyond one in 10^{50}—a much smaller figure than what we have been dealing with—is an event which we can state with certainty will *never* happen—no matter how much time is allotted, no matter how many conceivable opportunities could exist for the event to take place (Emile Borel, *Probabilities and Life* [New York: Dover, 1962], chapters one and three). In other words, life by chance is mathematically impossible on earth or any place else.

A rather humorous example will help us to understand the size of very large numbers. Suppose that an amoeba, that microscopic little creature, were given the job of moving the entire universe—the earth, the solar system, all the stars, all the galaxies etc., *one atom* at a time. He had to carry each atom across the entire universe, a distance of thirty billion light years (a light year is the distance light travels in a year going at the speed of 186,000 miles per second). To top it off, he had to carry these atoms at the incredibly slow traveling speed of one *inch* every fifteen billion years. If this amoeba, traveling one inch in fifteen billion years over such a vast distance, moved atom by atom not just one universe, but six hundred thousand trillion trillion trillion trillion universes the size of ours, the number of years it would take him would be "only" 10^{171} years (from James Coppedge, *Evolution: Possible or Impossible* [Grand Rapids: Zondervan, 1974] pp. 118–120). This is almost infinitely smaller than 10^{415}, the chance that for all practical purposes the universe could evolve one ap-

78

propriate DNA molecule necessary for a certain chemical reaction!

If you want a *really* big number, try calculating the chance of life *itself* evolving on just one planet, i.e., the earth. Doctor Carl Sagan of Cornell University estimated this to be roughly one chance in ten followed by two *billion* zeros (Carl Sagan, ed., *Communication With Extra-Terrestrial Intelligence*, MIT Press, 1973, p. 46). A number this large would fill over 6,000 books this size just to write it out. A number this size is so infinitely beyond 10^{50} (Borel's upper limit for an event to occur), it is simply mind boggling.

As scientists have faced the logical conclusions of their own research and theories, they have been slow to accept the implications. Doctor George Wald, Nobel prize-winning biologist of Harvard University, stated several years ago: "One only has to contemplate the magnitude of this task to concede that the spontaneous generation of a living organism is impossible. Yet here we are—as a result, I believe, of spontaneous generation" (Weldon took this from Henry Morris and John Whitcomb in *The Genesis Flood*. [Nutley, N.J.: Presbyterian and Reformed, 1971], p. 234). This statement might cause us to wonder about the rational thinking of so great a scientist. But a year earlier Dr. Wald stated what evidently was the real problem: "The reasonable view was to believe in spontaneous generation; the only alternative, to believe in a single, primary act of supernatural creation. There is no third position. For this reason many scientists a century ago chose to regard the belief in spontaneous generation as a philosophical necessity . . . . Most modern biologists, having viewed with satisfaction the downfall of the spontaneous generation hypothesis, yet unwilling to accept the alternative belief in special creation, are left with nothing."

The Bible and Alien Life

I asked Columbia Pictures' John Veitch if he believed there was life in outer space. "I really don't know," he answered. "I don't know if there's life on other planets. I feel if there is, the good Lord would have made some reference to it—maybe He has. But I'm not bright enough to have seen it in the Bible."

If there were intelligent beings with origins in outer space, we would expect the Bible to support the fact. However, the Bible takes no such position. In the first chapter of the Book of Genesis, we read the account of God's creation, but nowhere do we see the slightest hint about life being created on other worlds. Quite the contrary. Because elsewhere in the Bible, in Psalms 115:16, the heavens are pictured as belonging to God, while men are said to be exclusive to the earth. Again, no mention is made of life in outer space. Furthermore, the Bible doesn't even mention the existence of other planets. While some might exist, science has yet to locate planets in other solar systems. Most importantly, the person of Jesus Christ and His redemptive work underscore the uniqueness of life to the planet earth. He came to die for man's sins, exclusively.

Finally, in the last book of the Bible, the Book of Revelation, chapter twenty-one, we read that the entire universe, including earth, will be destroyed by God in the end. His believers will live with Him for all eternity in a new and different kind of world, and those who rejected His Son's Lordship and free gift of salvation, will spend eternity in total separation from Him. But still, no mention is made of other planets or extraterrestrial life.

The persistent questions remain: What are UFOs, and where do they come from?

7

Encountering Another Dimension

As Roy Neary and Jillian Guiler watched the heavens from their perch on the rocky slope of Devil's Tower, they saw a boiling cloud move across the sky, change direction, then come toward them! Out of the cloud appeared spheres of light which sped through the sky in a dazzling display of aerobatics. The luminous spheres "split" into multiple UFOs and buzzed Roy and Jillian and the landing pad at the foot of Devil's Tower.

The UFOs came rolling and tumbling through the air, passing close enough for Roy and Jillian to see that they appeared to be translucent, rather than solid.

And that's exactly the way the makers of *Close Encounters of the Third Kind* wanted their UFOs to look.

"We decided to work with light, suggesting, rather than showing, shapes," explained *Close Encounters'* special-photographic-effects wizard, Douglas Trumbull, in an interview with Gregg Kilday of the *Los Angeles Times*.

This approach taken by Trumbull and Spielberg was grounded in the fact that so many reports of UFO encounters describe the objects as "luminous" and "glowing." Remember that this was the very description given by President Carter in his reported close encounter.

Mechanical Difficulties

More and more UFOlogists are finding it difficult to hold to the "mechanical" theory of the nature of UFOs. In fact, some scientists, including Dr. J.

Allen Hynek and John A. Keel, seem to have totally abandoned the "visitors in flying saucers from other planets" theory. Instead, they offer other explanations for the UFO phenomenon.

Doctor Hynek, for one, now expounds a theory he calls "parallel reality." The astronomer explains it this way: "You and I know that there are television images passing through this room right now. But you'd have a hard time convincing an Australian aborigine of that.

"Or suppose you landed on an island where, for generations, everyone had been born congenitally blind. There is no way you could describe a red sunset to them. *That* would be a parallel reality for them.

"We know that there are a great many spaces within the atom which we cannot begin to see, even with an electron microscope. Those spaces are as vast, relatively, as the spaces between the stars in our solar system. What if those spaces represent an entire universe parallel to our own, implying that UFOs are a product of 'inner space' rather than 'outer space'?

"Parallel reality is one of many theories which cannot be confirmed or rejected until far more scientific data has been compiled and many more years of investigation and evaluation have been completed."

Other Dimensions

In a well-researched article in the *SCP Journal*, authors Mark Albrecht and Brooks Alexander, discuss this "parallel reality" and other dimensions in time and space. They quote John Keel from his thesis which tries to explain that UFOs are not permanent material objects, although they might seem to be solid:

"The statistical data," they quote Keel, ". . . indicate that flying saucers are *not* stable machines requiring fuel, maintenance, and logistical support. They are, in all probability, transmogrifications of energy and do not exist in the same way that this book exists. They are not permanent constructions of matter" (John A. Keel, *Operation Trojan Horse* [New York: G. P. Putnam and Sons, 1970], p. 182, as quoted by Mark Albrecht and Brooks Alexander, *SCP Journal*, August 1977, p. 20).

Transmogrification isn't a term you might use every day! It simply means "a strange or grotesque change in appearance or form."

Doctor Curt Wagner, a physicist whose doctoral degree is in the field of general relativity theory, agrees with Keel's assessment. Doctor Wagner, quoted in the August 1977 issue of *SCP Journal* said, "Drawing from what we know can happen in séances and poltergeist activity, it seems that these supernatural forces can manipulate matter and energy, extracting energy from the atmosphere, for example (which manifests as a local temperature change), to manipulate matter and produce an apparent violation of the second law (of thermodynamics), and I guess my feeling is that on a larger scale this is what a UFO could be. I'm not saying I know that it is, but only that it could be. It seems to me likely that UFOs are large-scale violations of the second law in which energy is arranged to take on enough of a force-field appearance so that it appears to look like matter, yet it's really just an energy concentration—it's not really solid matter in the usual sense."

The article went on to quote astrophysicist Jacques Vallee on the subject of UFOs that appear and disappear suddenly or change shape: "Everything seems to work as if these observers (of UFOs) had seen successive projections into our three-dimensional space of objects of a higher dimensionality."

The Fourth Dimension

What other dimension could there be? All of us are familiar with the three dimensions of length, width, and depth, but how many of us have ever seen (or perceived in some other way) a *fourth* dimension? When you get right down to it, none of us has really seen the first *three* dimensions in their true perspective. Now let me explain that. We don't see all three dimensions of length, width, and depth at once.

Imagine you are looking at the side of a child's building block from straight on. What do you see? Height and width, that's all—you can't see depth. You know the block has depth, however, because you saw its other sides before.

We basically see only two dimensions, and the third one is *inferred*. We see only two dimensions on a motion-picture screen, for example, but our minds infer a third dimension.

Can we see a *fourth* dimension? If Dr. Curt Wagner is correct in his theory that UFOs are forms of pure energy which become visible, then they evidently are becoming visible within the three dimensions with which we are familiar. But Hynek believes UFOs are of a parallel reality, and Vallee agrees that they must be of a higher dimension (higher than the familiar three).

If we actually see only two dimensions and our

minds infer the third, then why couldn't our minds infer a fourth dimension? Sounds good—in theory. But what would we be looking at? What is the fourth dimension? Hynek, Keel, and others will only say that the fourth dimension could be the realm in which UFOs operate, and that they become visible to us in dimensions we can perceive for some unknown reasons.

Other scientists believe *time* is the fourth dimension. Adding to the confusion are some who say there is a fourth dimension—then a fifth one, a sixth, a seventh, and so on! Finally, there is a group which holds that there are many aspects to the fourth dimension, time being only one of them.

The Spirit Realm

Unfortunately, science hasn't helped much in giving any understanding to the fourth dimension or to the origin and nature of UFOs.

The investigative efforts of many scientists point to the reality of UFOs, yet "real" in a way they cannot define. UFOs, they theorize, are of another dimension, but it is a dimension they haven't begun to understand—or even agree upon, among themselves.

Perhaps they have been looking in the wrong field of study for the answers. Perhaps they should investigate *theology*. I think they would find it a better base of knowledge for understanding the fourth dimension.

They could start by reading the Bible. It tells of another "realm" of existence—another dimension, if you will—the spirit world, the world of the supernatural. This is the dimension—the supernatural realm—of God and His angels, and of Satan and his demons (which are "fallen" angels).

The Bible describes God as a single, divine, spirit being. He is a personality who possesses unlimited powers and knowledge. His character is flawless. By Himself, He created the earth, the sun—the entire universe, and all that is. Because God is a personality, He can relate with human beings on a personal level. He does this through the other two personalities of the Holy Trinity—His Son, Jesus Christ, and His Holy Spirit.

Satan, who originally was called Lucifer, on the other hand, was the most beautiful *created* being in all of God's Kingdom. Satan even ranked above all the other created beings in heaven. But he willed in his heart to become greater than God, and this transgression led to his downfall. The Bible tells us that Satan was subsequently cast down from heaven—but not before he deceived a third of the angels, convincing them to join the rebellion. Consequently, all of these rebel angels were thrown out of heaven along with Satan.

The Bible presents a broad panorama of world history which shows that the conflict of Satan and his demons against God and His angels will continue until the end of the world as we know it. At that time, God will destroy Satan and his demons, as well as the heavens and the earth. Then, He will replace it all with a new world of eternal bliss for believers and a place of everlasting torment for those who rejected His Son, Jesus Christ.

The theory that UFOs are of the spirit realm is not new. In the next chapter we will see how some writers have attempted to relate UFOs with religion by showing that God was a UFOnaut, while in the chapter after that, we will examine the similarities between UFOs and the occult.

Part 3

*Encountering the
New Space-Age
Religions*

8

Was God a UFOnaut?

As *Close Encounters of the Third Kind* reaches its climax, a number of people, including an ecstatic Roy Neary, are being prepared to board the mother spacecraft for a flight to their "haven of everlasting salvation."

Only minutes before, a group of navy pilots had stepped off the craft. They appeared to be just as young as when they had mysteriously vanished during World War II! Just seeing them caused Roy to sense that he was about to travel into—immortality!

At the impromptu chapel service, the chanting of the priest only confirmed what lay ahead for Roy: "By the guidance of a star, grant these pilgrims, we pray, a happy journey and peaceful days so that with Your divine angel as their guide, they may reach their destination and finally come to the haven of everlasting salvation" (Steven Spielberg, *Close Encounters,* pp. 247, 248).

A Chariot of the Gods?

What is this? What are we being told to believe? Is this a space vehicle that could transport humans into immortality, to everlasting salvation? Is it sanctioned by God and guided by angels? Where does reality leave off and science fiction begin? Where does Christianity end and the new space-age religion start? Is God a UFOnaut? Sadly, some apostles of the gospel according to science fiction believe that He is. But long before *Close Encounters* began broadcasting its special brand of theology, there were other voices crying in the wilderness.

Starting in the late 1960s, German author Erich von Daniken fascinated millions of people with his international best-selling book, *Chariots of the Gods*. In his book he states: "I claim that our forefathers received visits from the universe in the remote past, even though I do not yet know who these extraterrestrial intelligences were or from which planet they came. I nevertheless proclaim that these 'strangers' annihilated part of mankind existing at the time and produced a new, perhaps the first, *homo sapiens*" (Erich von Daniken, *Chariots of the Gods* [New York: Bantam, 1971], p. x).

Inspired by von Daniken's book, Josef F. Blumrich, chief of the systems-layout branch of NASA, wrote the book, *The Spaceships of Ezekiel*. Blumrich's book is based on the results of technical studies which "show us a space vehicle which beyond any doubt is not only technically feasible but in fact is very well designed to fulfill its functions and purpose . . . . Moreover, the results indicate a spaceship operated in conjunction with a mother spacecraft orbiting the earth" (Josef F. Blumrich, *The Spaceships of Ezekiel* [New York: Bantam, 1974], p. 3).

Ancestors in Outer Space?

Von Daniken and others apparently believe that we humans are the offspring of ancient astronauts and that our oldest ancestors came from outer space.

The eminent Nobel-prize-winner, Dr. Francis Crick, theorized that life on earth might have originated from a spore of life planted long ago by some outer-space civilization. Addressing this theory, author John Weldon states, "This type of reasoning is due mostly to the fact that some scientists are having increasing difficulties believing that life could arise by chance. If however, life was planted here, this supposedly solves the problem. In reality it doesn't solve anything—it just pushes the question back a notch. Where did the life that created us then come from? At some point in the past, life had to have originated by chance, and then we are back where we started with our original question—where did life come from?

"There is one question, however, that is answered by this type of reasoning," Weldon continues. "It shows how far even brilliant men will go to escape the idea of God being their Creator" (Weldon, *UFO's*, pp. 156, 157).

Have we entered an age of irrationality? Paul Kurtz, head of the Committee for the Scientific Investigation of Claims of the Paranormal, believes our nation is being caught up in a retreat from reason. Citing *Close Encounters*, he says the movie house has become the sacred church for pseudo-scientific faiths. Why is it that so many people are choosing to let belief in the obvious become replaced by a belief in the impossible?

A Religious Need

Doctor Carl Sagan of the Department of Astronomy at Harvard University and the Smithsonian Astrophysical Observatory believes this surging wave of irrationality stems from religious needs which are not being found in the institutional religions:

"The interest in unidentified flying objects derives, perhaps, not so much from scientific curiosity as from unfulfilled religious needs. Flying saucers serve, for some, to replace the gods that science has deposed. With their distant and exotic worlds and their pseudoscientific overlay, the contact accounts are acceptable to many people who reject the older religious frameworks. But precisely because people desire so intensely that unidentified flying objects be of benign, intelligent, and extraterrestrial origin, honesty requires that, in evaluating the observations, we accept only the most rigorous logic and the most convincing evidence. At the present time, there is no evidence that unambiguously connects the various flying saucer sightings and contact tales with extraterrestrial intelligence" (*Encyclopedia Americana* [New York: Grolier Inc., 1967]).

Why is it that people place such faith and hope in speculation about the origins and purposes of UFOs?

The *SCP Journal* points out that the skies have long held a fascination and a fear for the inhabitants of earth. According to a recent article, the magazine said, "Studies in archaeology and anthropology have shown that 'the idea which regards the sky as the abode of the Supreme Being, or as identical with Him, is as universal among mankind as any religious belief can be, and is traceable back to the most primitive stages of culture known to us' " (*SCP Journal*, August 1977, p. 12, with quote from Edwyn Bevan, *Symbolism and Belief* [Boston: Beacon Press, 1957], p. 48).

The Uniqueness of Man

Man looks at himself, the world around him, and to the skies above, and repeats those persistent questions: Did man originate by chance from life-less matter? Or are we the children of ancient as-tronauts from outer space? Or were we created by God? The Bible gives the answer, in God's words: "It is I who made the earth, and created man upon it. I stretched out the heavens with My hands, and I ordained all their host" (Isaiah 45:12 NAS).

The creation account in the Book of Genesis shows that God created man with a supreme place in the universe. Man is given charge over the earth and all the other creatures (*see* Genesis 1:27–2:3; cf. Amos 4:13; Isaiah 42:5; Psalms 8:4–6; Hebrews 2).

The Bible repeatedly emphasizes that man is a part of nature—an animal, if you will. But man's purpose cannot be found in the lowly nature of typi-cal animals. Instead, man has God's prophetic his-tory to live and destiny to fulfill.

"God created man in His own image . . ." (Genesis 1:27 NAS). He created man with body, to be sure, and with spirit and soul. Man's soul is his innermost being—his will, intellect, and emotions. Through his spirit, man can relate to God. Original sin broke that spiritual relationship between God and man, but Jesus' atoning sacrifice for the sins of all people restores that relationship, provided one becomes spiritually "born again" through receiving Jesus Christ by faith as Saviour and Lord. Only through receiving Christ can man know God and relate to God in His divine image.

The Sons of God and the Daughters of Men

In *Chariots of the Gods* Erich von Daniken offers a space-age-religion interpretation of Genesis 6:1, 2 in an effort to support his theory that man has origins in outer space. The passage reads: "Now it came about, when men began to multiply on the face of the land, and daughters were born to them, that the sons of God saw that the daughters of men were beautiful; and they took wives for themselves, whomever they chose" (NAS).

Von Daniken asks: "Who can tell us what sons of God took the daughters of men to wife? Ancient Israel had a single sacrosanct God. Where do the 'sons of God' come from?" (von Daniken, *Chariots of the Gods,* p. 34). He goes on to state that the "sons of God" must be beings from outer space who came to earth and interbred with human beings. But there are difficulties with his interpretation. First, the Bible certainly doesn't present such a view. Second, von Daniken bases his theory on the presupposition that intelligent life originated in outer space. But the existence of such beings has never been proven.

If von Daniken's theory isn't valid, then what is the true meaning of "sons of God" and the rest of these verses?

There are some Bible scholars who believe that Genesis 6:4 refers to fallen angelic beings who took on physical bodies and went around lusting after women and having immoral relations with them. The offspring of such unions, according to this view are the *Nephilim* or "giants" mentioned in Genesis 6:4.

Other Bible scholars believe that the passage refers to the godly line of Seth ("sons of God") which married into the ungodly line of Cain ("daughters of men"). Those who take this interpretation point out that the phrase, "took wives for themselves" (Genesis 6:2) is a customary biblical expression used to describe a marriage. Nowhere in the Bible is the phrase used to describe intimate relations outside of marriage.

Furthermore, the Bible does not indicate that the Nephilim are the offspring of marriages between the "sons of God" and the "daughters of men." Certainly, therefore, they are not the illegitimate offspring of immoral unions between men from outer space and women of this planet, as von Daniken theorizes.

Who then are the Nephilim? They are simply men who existed in those days and in days afterward. Too much should not be read into the reference to giants, since these Nephilim are simply said to be men of literally "great size" (*see* Numbers 13:33).

Christian Bible scholars may differ on whether "sons of God" are fallen angels who have relations with women or whether they are godly men who marry women of an ungodly line. But the Bible, without question, does not support von Daniken's theory of interbreeding among alien beings and humans. Furthermore, neither the "sons of God" nor God Himself are implied in the Bible to be UFOnauts from outer space.

One of the most popular schemes to support the theory that God was a UFOnaut is to concoct a close encounter by the prophet Ezekiel and a UFO, based upon a vision recorded in the Old Testament.

Erich von Daniken devotes several pages of his book *Chariots of the Gods* to the theory that Ezekiel saw a spaceship piloted by strange, alien beings. This theory is expanded by NASA engineer, Josef F. Blumrich in his book, *The Spaceships of Ezekiel.*

The Book of Ezekiel starts with the appearance of the Lord before him, calling him to service as a prophet. Following is the passage, exactly as von Daniken quotes it:

Now it came to pass in the thirtieth year, in the fourth month, in the fifth day of the month, as I was among the captives by the river of Chebar, that the heavens were opened . . . . And I looked, and, behold, a whirlwind came out of the north, a great cloud, and a fire infolding itself, and a brightness was about it, and out of the midst thereof as the colour of amber, out of the midst of the fire. Also out of the midst thereof came the likeness of four living creatures. And this was their appearance; they had the likeness of a man. And every one had four faces, and every one had four wings. And their feet were straight feet; and the sole of their feet was like the sole of a calf's foot: and they sparkled like the colour of burnished brass.

Ezekiel 1:1, 4–7 KJV

Von Daniken then states that these verses give "precise details" of the landing of a spaceship.

98

Von Daniken goes on to ask, "Who spoke to Ezekiel?" Interestingly, von Daniken omitted the very portion from that passage in Ezekiel 1 that answers that very question! Here are verses 1–3, but with the portions omitted by von Daniken put back in, in italics:

Now it came to pass in the thirtieth year, in the fourth month, in the fifth day of the month, as I was among the captives by the river of Chebar, that the heavens were opened, *and I saw visions of God. In the fifth day of the month, which was the fifth year of King Jehoiachin's captivity, The word of the Lord came expressly unto Ezekiel the priest, the son of Buzi, in the land of the Chaldeans by the river Chebar; and the hand of the Lord was there upon him.*"

Ezekiel 1:1–3 KJV

So, to answer von Daniken's question, "Who spoke to Ezekiel?" we find the answer in that portion of Scripture omitted from von Daniken's quote: *God*, Himself, spoke to Ezekiel!

The priest Ezekiel had seen a "vision of God" by the river Chebar, and there, "The hand of the Lord came upon him." God spoke to Ezekiel—and no one else heard Him talking, because Ezekiel writes that "The word of the Lord came *expressly* unto Ezekiel."

The word *vision* is translated from the Hebrew word *murah*. This word comes from the ordinary root *to see*, and means a vision "as a means of revelation."

Such visions as Ezekiel's are not necessarily meant to be taken literally, for example, another vision of Ezekiel's, in which Israel's future rebirth as a nation was seen as dry bones which became covered with flesh and skin to live again (*see* Ezekiel 37). Likewise, this vision was symbolic in that God was revealing Himself to a people in need of Him.

God had sought to come to Ezekiel to reveal certain truths about Himself and His plans for the people of Israel and the rest of the world. And how Ezekiel and his countrymen needed such encouragement! It was six hundred years before the birth of Jesus Christ. Jerusalem, the holy city of God, was decaying because of the oppression imposed upon them by the despised Babylonians. The bitter irony was that King Nebuchadnezzar's godless, sinful Babylon was living in high luxury. Ezekiel was never initiated as a priest because of the occupation and his people had been reduced to wallowing in the problems of their oppression and meager existence.

The Israelites needed God, and He came to them in their time of need—through a vision given to the prophet Ezekiel: "The word of the Lord came [to me] . . . and the hand of the Lord was there upon [me] . . ." (Ezekiel 1:3 KJV).

Von Daniken's UFO

So Ezekiel *knew* God was speaking to him through a vision. It was a vision of a whirling, powerful wind that somehow generated a strange cloud that was illuminated with brilliant flashes of light and a burning intensity that gave the appearance of glowing brass.

100

Von Daniken and Blumrich have *literally* interpreted portions of Ezekiel's vision and *symbolically* interpreted others in a way to suggest that Ezekiel had seen a spaceship. Certainly, such a visitation by God, sadly, could be misinterpreted as a UFO. And, that being the situation with von Daniken and Blumrich, the whole significance of this fascinating passage of Scripture has been missed by them.

God was describing Himself to Ezekiel through this vision. God was rushing about, like a fresh and mighty wind—unseen, but certainly noticed! God was reminding Ezekiel that He was the same God who, like a mighty wind, swept over the surface of the waters at the beginning of creation (*see* Genesis 1:2). God's appearance as a swirling, fiery cloud let the young prophet know, too, that this was a revelation of the same God who had appeared to Ezekiel's forefathers in the form of the cloud by day and the pillar of fire by night (*see* Exodus 13:21, 22). Such an appearance by God is called by a technical term, *theophany*.

The fiery cloud surely reminded Ezekiel of Moses' description of God as being, among other things, ". . . a consuming fire, even a jealous God" (Deuteronomy 4:24 KJV; cf. Hebrews 12:29). The "fiery brass" reminds us that the Lord's feet are seen as brass glowing in a furnace in Revelation 1:15, which symbolizes the magnificence and strength of the Lord (George E. Ladd, *Revelation* [Grand Rapids: Eerdmans, 1972], p. 33).

Through the prophet Ezekiel, the captive Israelites at Tel-abib would soon be told to look again with reverence to their mighty God as the source of strength in their time of trial.

The Four Living Creatures

But there is more, much more to Ezekiel's vision, than meets the eye of some beholders!

"Also out of the midst thereof came the likeness of four living creatures," Ezekiel went on to say. "And this was their appearance; they had the likeness of a man. And every one had four faces, and every one had four wings. And their feet were straight feet; and the sole of their feet was like the sole of a calf's foot: and they sparkled like the colour of burnished brass" (Ezekiel 1:5–7 KJV).

Once again von Daniken leaves out key portions of the passage he quotes. This time, he omits mention of verses 8–13, apparently preferring to sidestep trying to fit the four living creatures described there into his theory. However, Blumrich sees the four living creatures as four helicopter attachments to a spaceship that is making a landing approach on planet earth. But what do the four living creatures represent in view of biblical symbolism? First, let's look at verses 8–13:

Under their wings on their four sides were human hands. As for the faces and wings of the four of them, their wings touched one another; their faces did not turn when they moved, each went straight forward. As for the form of their faces, each had the face of a man, all four had the face of a lion on the right and the face of a bull on the left, and all four had the face of an eagle. Such were their faces. Their wings were spread out above; each had two touching another being, and two covering their bodies. And each went straight forward; wherever the spirit was about to go, they would go, without

102

turning as they went. In the midst of the living beings there was something that looked like burning coals of fire, like torches darting back and forth among the living beings. The fire was bright, and lightning was flashing from the fire.

NAS

Each creature had four faces—man, lion, ox, and eagle. Their significance, according to the old rabbis, is said to be that man is the greatest of all created beings, the lion the greatest among the wild animals, the ox, the greatest domestic beast, and the eagle, the greatest among the birds (Stuart Briscoe, *All Things Weird and Wonderful* [Wheaton, IL: Victor Books, 1977], p. 15).

These four living creatures, though variously described, are mentioned several times in the Bible, including Ezekiel 10:14; Revelation 4:6.

Doctor George E. Ladd, the author of many commentaries on the Bible and professor at Fuller Theological Seminary in California, comments that these four living creatures "may be interpreted in two different ways. Either the cherubim (four living creatures) represent the praise and adoration extended to the Creator by the totality of His creation; or else they represent angelic beings who are used by the Creator in executing His rule and His divine will in all the orders of His creation. They are created spirits who are thought of as mediating the divine energy and power in all the world. The fact that they sing a song of adoration, 'Holy, holy, holy, is the Lord God Almighty, who was and is and is to come!,' suggests that both interpretations may be correct" (Ladd, *Revelation*, p. 77).

103

Stuart Briscoe, in his interesting commentary on Ezekiel, writes that the vision was preparing the prophet for his ministry by showing the Lord to him and by reminding him about the things God expects to see in those whom He uses:

First, "they had the likeness of a man" (1:5) which reminds us that of all the created orders, *humanity* is the one the Lord uses primarily for His purposes.

Second, "their feet were straight feet" (1:7) which speaks of the necessity for *stability* in the work of the Lord.

Third, "they sparkled like the color of burnished brass" (1:7), a clear reference to their *purity*.

Fourth, "they had the hands of a man under their wings" (1:8), which graphically points out that the Lord's work requires people with a sense of *practicality* to go with their wings!

Fifth, "their wings were stretched upward" (1:11), which portrays a great sense of urgency and *mobility*.

Sixth, "two wings covered their bodies" (1:11), demonstrating their *humility*.

Seventh, "they went every one straight forward" (1:12) which means that they had a great sense of purpose and commitment and moved with purpose and *integrity*.

Eighth, "whither the Spirit was to go they went" (1:12) is the great statement of their *availability*.

Ninth, "their appearance was like burning coals of fire" (1:13) describes their *intensity*.

Tenth, "they ran and returned as the appearance of a flash of lightning" (1:14) gives a tremendous sense of their *activity*.

This is an awesome picture of the ministry of God. Ezekiel was being shown in glorious technicolor that God moves in our world through His created beings and that His service is both the most exhilarating and terrifying activity in which humanity can be involved. (Briscoe, *All Things Weird and Wonderful*, p. 16.)

The Wheels With Eyes

Von Daniken, and Blumrich especially, make much of the mention of "wheels" in Ezekiel 1:15–21:

Now as I looked at the living beings, behold, there was one wheel on the earth beside the living beings, for each of the four of them. The appearance of the wheels and their workmanship was like sparkling beryl, and all four of them had the same form, their appearance and workmanship being as if one wheel were within another. Whenever they moved, they moved in any of their four directions, without turning as they moved. As for their rims they were lofty and awesome, and rims of all four of them were full of eyes round about. And whenever the living beings moved, the wheels moved with them. And whenever the living beings rose from the earth, the wheels rose also. Wherever the spirit was about to go, they would go in that direction. And the wheels rose close

105

beside them; for the spirit of the living beings was in the wheels. Whenever those went, these went; and whenever those stood still, these stood still. And whenever those rose from the earth, the wheels rose close beside them; for the spirit of the living beings was in the wheels.

NAS

Von Daniken interprets these wheels as those similar to today's all-terrain recreational vehicles, while Blumrich goes to great technical explanation of a mechanical type of wheel which he believes functions in accordance with the description in Ezekiel.

Briscoe points out that Ezekiel is simply saying that the wheels symbolize God's ability to "get anywhere He wants to at anytime and, if necessary, move in four directions simultaneously! The technical word for what he saw is 'omnipresence.'"

Briscoe goes on to point out that Ezekiel then noticed the *size* of the wheels. John Taylor is quoted in giving a literal translation of Ezekiel's words: "As for their rims, height to them and fear to them."

"In other words," explains Briscoe, Ezekiel "was overwhelmed with the sheer size and immensity of the movement of God . . . . Their power was awesome. Here the technical word is 'omnipotence'" (Briscoe, *All Things Weird and Wonderful*, p. 17).

Ezekiel then described the strangest feature about the wheels: the rims were "full of eyes." Briscoe refers to another passage in Scripture which states that "the eyes of the Lord run to and fro throughout the whole earth . . ." (2 Chronicles 16:9 KJV). This simply means that nothing is hidden from

God's view. He knows our innermost thoughts and desires. This "all-knowing" characteristic of God is called *omniscience*.

Spirit Power

While von Daniken and Blumrich believe Ezekiel's vehicle is powered by some heat-producing machinery, the Bible text explains that the wheels and the four living creatures are motivated by the Spirit of God—spirit power, if you will: "Whithersoever the spirit was to go, they went . . . for the spirit of the living creature was in the wheels" (Ezekiel 1:20 KJV). God is seen here in complete control of all living creatures and all inanimate things, which are used to reveal His unlimited power, total knowledge, and ever presence.

The Throne of God

How would you begin to describe God as He sits seated upon His throne? Well, this is the picture Ezekiel saw in his vision, and Ezekiel obviously could not find words to adequately convey the wondrous sight before him. Nonetheless, he described this wonderful sight in the best way he possibly could, likening the platform upon which the throne rested as looking like a sheet of ice, awe inspiring, (*see* 1:22).

Ezekiel saw what appeared to be a kind of sapphire in the shape resembling a throne, and on this throne was a humanlike form (*see* 1:26). But it was not a human, because it had what had the godly brilliance of brass glowing like fire in a furnace from the waist upward. And, from the waist down, the form looked like encircling radiance—like a "rainbow in the clouds on a rainy day, so was the appearance of the surrounding radiance. Such was the appearance of the likeness of the glory of the Lord . . ." (1:28 NAS).

Ezekiel then fell on his face as God spoke to him, saying, ". . .'Son of man, I am sending you to the sons of Israel, to a rebellious people who have rebelled against Me; they and their fathers have transgressed against Me to this very day. And I am sending you to them who are stubborn and obstinate children; and you shall say to them, "Thus says the Lord God." As for them, whether they listen or not—for they are a rebellious house—they will know that a prophet has been among them' " (2:3–5 NAS).

God revealed Himself in all His mysterious majesty to an ancient Hebrew by the name of Ezekiel, calling him to be a prophet to minister to his people. The same God of Ezekiel is revealing Himself to people today, through His creation, through the Bible, through Jesus Christ, through modern Ezekiels, and through His Spirit which speaks directly to the hearts of men. Sadly, many people misinterpret these revelations, just as some see only meaningless spaceships on the pages of the Book of Ezekiel. We can be thankful that God is not a UFOnaut, and that what Ezekiel saw and recorded was more than a piece of machinery.

9

Close Encounters With the Occult

Roy Neary was driving his wife, Ronnie, crazy with his incessant talk about the UFOs. It was all he could think about. And then he began getting mental flashes of some odd-shaped form. The first one came when he was shaving one morning. He squirted a mound of Rapid Shave into the palm of his hand, and the sight of it captured his attention. There was something strangely familiar about that shape, but his mind just could not make the connection.

Roy experienced something similar to that feeling you have when you think you are doing something you have done before, but know you didn't do it. Weird feeling, isn't it?

Well this strange sensation of Roy's didn't just happen once, then go away: It happened over and over again. The next time he sensed the mystifying form was when his eye caught a rumpled pillow on the bed. He saw it once more in a plate full of mashed potatoes!

Ronnie's Cover-up

Ronnie was so embarrassed by Roy and his crazy talk about UFOs that she even wanted to lie to their friends about his UFO-burned cheek, telling them it was caused when he fell asleep under a sunlamp on his right side.

Ronnie wasn't the only person concerned about the UFO stories that Roy was spreading about town. Grimsby called from the department and told Ronnie that Roy had been fired. That's all, just fired. They hadn't even wanted to talk with Roy directly. And it was all because of his talk about UFOs.

The loss of his job didn't deter Roy from his preoccupation with UFOs. He plastered the walls of his house with press clippings and sketches he had drawn. And then he began to sculpt "it" right there in his living room! Dirt, junk—everything he could pick up or tear loose—went into the project. It created quite an uproar in the neighborhood, to say the least.

Ronnie had had it. She could stand it no longer. Convinced that Roy had gone completely bananas, she loaded the kids and herself into the family station wagon and peeled off to find refuge at her mother's.

Meanwhile, Jillian had set up a makeshift art studio in a corner of her living room, where she agonizingly whiled away her time, waiting for word from the authorities about Barry. Strangely, she felt compelled to sketch a form of some sort which would almost come into focus in her mind, but then fade away.

Jillian was receiving the same "message" as Roy!

The Beckoning

The mystery became partially solved when the evening news came on TV. The top story concerned a train derailment in Wyoming. A tanker car carrying the highly toxic G-M nerve gas ruptured, according to the report, causing the entire region to be evacuated.

The purported accident occurred not far from the majestic Devil's Tower, a granite peak that soared high into the sky. Roy, almost by accident, spotted

110

the TV report while he was sculpting in his living room. Jillian, meanwhile, caught it on another news program while she sketched. Both of them immediately recognized Devil's Tower as the "thing" they had been trying to bring into focus in their minds.

The drive to build the "thing," which had brought Roy near the brink of a nervous breakdown, began to make sense. He wasn't crazy after all. There was a message, somewhere, in all of this. He was being summoned to Devil's Tower! Why, he didn't know. He just had to get there, fast!

Jillian, too, felt the beckoning of Devil's Tower. She was almost beside herself with the joyful expectation of finding Barry there.

What was this strange force that was communicating with their minds, manipulating their thoughts? Was it good? Or was it evil? Late in the film, it is implied that God is behind all this. But is this the same God of the Bible?

The "God" of the New Space-Age Religion

According to the science-fiction gospel of Hollywood's newest prophets, God is neither good nor evil. Instead, God is seen as being a very impersonal, infinite power. Whether that power is exercised for good or evil purposes depends upon the user. In order to tap this power, a person must learn the proper techniques. Unfortunately, those techniques are usually quite ambiguous, and vary greatly from one motion picture to another. And, they contradict biblical teachings.

In *Close Encounters,* Roy responds to the telepathic messages of this infinite power in the wrong way. He almost goes nuts, and then loses his job and his family in the process of discovering the mystery behind Devil's Tower and the UFOs.

The sensational science-fantasy epic *Star Wars* gives us a number of excellent examples of people who tap the powers of the infinite force to use it for either good or evil purposes. Darth Vader, the dark lord of the sith who wore a grotesque breathing mask and a Nazitype black helmet, got his kicks out of harnessing the power of the force to do evil. In this way, he is said to have mastered the ways of the "dark side" of the force. The film's hero, Luke Skywalker, on the other hand, was instructed by the venerable Obi-Wan Kenobi in the ways of the force to do good, not evil.

It is the same infinite force, just different applications of its power.

The theory of an infinite power that is neither good nor evil is also popular among several of today's science-fiction writers who grope for a connection between God, Satan, and beings from outer space or another dimension. John Keel expresses this common view in his book, *The Eighth Tower:* "If you had dared to suggest one hundred years ago that God and the devil were in cahoots, you would be invited to attend a barbecue in the public square, and you would be the barbecuee. But today it is apparent that the same force that answers some prayers also causes it to rain anchovies and is behind everything from sea serpents to flying saucers. It distorts our reality whimsically, perhaps out of boredom, or perhaps because it is a little crazy.

"God may be a crackpot" (Keel, *The Eighth Tower* [New York: Saturday Review Press, 1976], p. 20).

This, of course, is where the gospel of the new

space-age religion contradicts the Bible. According to the Bible, the Kingdom of God and the domain of the devil are totally different and totally separate from one another. The Kingdom of God can be described by God's own attributes, among them, love, joy, peace, goodness, righteousness, and so on. The devil, or Satan, opposes God and His attributes, and is said in the Scriptures to be a liar, a deceiver, and a blasphemer of God, among other things.

Close Encounters of the Third Kind gave us a fleet of UFOs, apparently sent by God to planet earth to select certain people and return with them to some undisclosed destination. In this regard, the movie differs from both the vast amount of literature on the nature of UFOs as well as the biblical teachings on the nature of God.

If, as the film implies, God is neither good nor bad, then we would expect his "messengers"—the UFOs—to be neither good nor bad. However, the UFOs did cause evil things to happen. People were frightened. There was at least one abduction (Barry Guiler). There was a massive power outage that was costly and inconvenient to people in many ways. Roy Neary almost went insane. Jillian Guiler experienced the emotional anguish of having her only child kidnapped. Citizens began to distrust their governing officials. Physical damage was done to the Guiler house and to Roy's DWP truck. Police cars were wrecked. The government lied to the people about the phony toxic-gas catastrophe. Roy lost his job and his wife and was alienated from his friends and neighbors. No doubt the list could be expanded.

Incredibly, all of these problems and evil events were completely forgotten when the moment ar-

113

rived for the UFOs to make contact with the earth-lings.

The UFOs of *Close Encounters* are hardly neutral—neither good nor evil. They did nothing but create problems for Roy and everyone else. But in the end these UFOnauts were looked upon with great awe—almost to the point of being worshiped!

UFOs and the Occult

We have examined some of the experts' opinions on the nature and origin of UFOs and have found little support for the theory that UFOs are mechanical spacecraft piloted by alien beings, or for the one that says they are secret weapons being tested by our government or someone else's. UFOs have been reported to have many shapes and sizes. Their occupants have been just as variously described—some as giants, others as midgets. Even in *Close Encounters of the Third Kind* there are several "specimens" of UFOnauts.

The governments of the world have so far been unable to give an adequate explanation of UFOs. All of this, coupled with the strange behavior of UFOs as found in the vast literature on the subject, indicates that we are dealing with a phenomenon which lies outside the normal field of *natural* events. This suggests that we should then investigate the *supernatural* realm for clues to the mysteries surrounding UFOs. For, of all the concepts we have dealt with so far, only the one that attributes UFOs to the activities of demons remains at all likely.

A surprising number of UFO researchers conclude that UFOs appear closely related to the occult. Lynn E. Catoe, the senior bibliographer for the

Library of Congress publication, *UFO's and Related Subjects: An Annotated Bibliography,* makes this significant statement in the introduction to the book:

"A large part of the available UFO literature is closely linked with mysticism and the metaphysical. It deals with subjects like mental telepathy, automatic writing, and invisible entities, as well as phenomena like poltergeist (ghost) manifestations and (demon) 'possession' . . . .

"Many of the UFO reports now being published in the popular press recount alleged incidents that are strikingly similar to demoniac possession and psychic phenomena which has long been known to theologians and parapsychologists" (*UFO's and Related Subjects: An Annotated Bibliography* [Washington: D.C.: U.S. Government Printing Office, 1969], p. iv, quoted by Weldon, *UFO's,* p. 95).

John Keel, in his widely read book *Operation Trojan Horse,* presents the view that, "Many flying saucers seem to be nothing more than a disguise for some hidden phenomenon. They are like trojan horses descending into our forests and farm fields, promising salvation and offering us the splendor of some great super civilization in the sky" (Keel, *Operation Trojan Horse,* p. 47).

Elsewhere in his book, Keel points out that the contents of many UFO messages are "identical to the messages long received by mediums and mystics." He goes on to explain that "demonology is not just another crackpot-ology. It is the ancient and scholarly study of monsters and demons who have seemingly coexisted with man throughout history. Thousands of books have been written on the subject, many of them authored by educated clergymen, scientists, and scholars, and uncounted numbers of well-documented demonic events are readily available to every researcher. The manifestations and occurrences described in this imposing literature are similar, if not entirely identical, to the UFO phenomenon itself. Victims of demonomania (demon possession) suffer the very same medical and emotional symptoms as the UFO contactees" (Keel, *Operation Trojan Horse,* p. 215).

Antichristian Behavior

The test of whether demons are behind the UFO phenomenon lies in the nature of UFO behavior. Reports of evil, antichristian activities on the part of UFOs have been passed on to us for centuries, only to be on the increase in our own time. If demons are behind the UFO phenomenon, then they are being directed by Satan himself. The Bible calls Satan a liar, slanderer, and murderer. He is a deceiver, and he has the ability to disguise himself as an "angel of light" (*see* 2 Corinthians 11:14). In this way, Satan and his demons can appear to be friendly spirits, while their intent is set on doing evil.

That is the way it was in *Close Encounters of the Third Kind.* The UFOs had brought havoc upon the town of Muncie, Indiana. But, then, at the end of the film, the UFOs appeared as angels of light, appearing to bring salvation and a utopian kind of world somewhere out in space.

Obviously, had Roy Neary, Claude Lacombe, and the others who participated in the close encounter with the mother spacecraft been up on their Bible studies, they would have known that salvation comes only through receiving Christ by faith, and not from UFOnauts!

116

Author John Weldon lists a few of the other lies and antichristian aspects of UFOnauts' behavior: "Saturn's civilizations exist in subtropical paradises; Venus has forests, streams, healthy wheat fields, suburban areas, etc.; the sun and Mercury are not hot, and Pluto is not cold, etc. They have said man will never be permitted to set foot on the moon, and have been ignorant of the earth's diameter and basic planetary physics. They have also espoused racist propaganda, particularly against the Jews; urged LSD and drug use and condoned premarital sex. They have made errors of judgment, knowledge and common sense that are absurd and continually espoused the beliefs of occultism, eastern religions and liberal theology. Seemingly without exception they deny the historic Christian faith. They claim to come from every planet in the solar system and then some" (Weldon, *UFO's*, p. 147).

Weldon cites as a classic example of deception the 2,000-page *Urantia Book*, supposedly authored by twenty-three persons who identify themselves as extraterrestrials. Weldon says of this book, "A full third is devoted to an unbiblical interpretation of the life, nature and death of Christ. It denies nearly every Christian belief and has a number of errors—historical, literary, and scientific. In a matter of hours I was able to list over one hundred statements in opposition to Biblical Christianity" (ibid. p. 148).

Escape From Urantia

Doctor Robert L. Hymers, Jr., pastor of the Open Door Community Church in Los Angeles, writes about what happened to one young man who read *Urantia Book:*

His eyes were glassy. His breath came in short gasps. Foam flecked the corners of his mouth. "Can I come in?" he finally gasped . . . .

"Come in, Don," I finally managed to say . . . .

"Pastor, you have to help me! You have to help me! No one else understands! No one else will believe me!" he moaned.

"Calm down, son," I spoke quietly. "Tell me about it."

I didn't know Don very well, in fact I'd only met him the night before, after the evening service. He had seemed a little confused then when he asked to counsel with me. I had told him to phone me later in the week, and had turned to some other pressing matter. But one of our perhaps overzealous young people had given him a book to read. The book explained how people can become demon-possessed through the occult.

Don clutched the book he had been given the night before, and he leaned forward in his chair . . . .

"What seems to be the trouble?" I asked.

"I've been reading this book all night. I know I'm demon-possessed. I know it!"

"How do you know?" I finally asked, amid the sounds of his crying.

"I tried to drive over to San Francisco. Something kept grabbing the wheel. Voices in my head kept saying, 'Drive off the road! Kill yourself!' I didn't know what to do, so I came here to you."

"Don, we need to have several counseling

118

sessions. Now if you'll phone me in the morning . . . ."

"Pastor, please pray for me! Please pray for me now! I'm going insane!" Beads of sweat stood out on his forehead.

"Sure, just be calm. Try to relax."

I closed my eyes and began, "Father, I pray that you'll give peace to Don. I pray that . . ." but I was stopped by a growling sound, like that of a vicious dog.

I opened my eyes just in time. Don was coming toward me, his fingers moving in a menacing way, his eyes wild, froth dribbling from his mouth. A horrible, vicious voice came from deep in his throat, "I'm going to kill you!"

I leaped from the chair and dashed to the other side of the room. One thought rushed through my mind, "He's dangerous, he's bigger than me, and I'm alone!" Then I did the only thing I could think of, I pointed my finger at the advancing figure and said, "Demon, I bind you in the name of Jesus Christ!" His body fell heavily to the floor at my feet.

In the next few minutes, as I bent in prayer over Don's writhing body, he began to grow calm. Finally he looked up at me. "I feel better now, Pastor," he said. So did I! (R. L. Hymers, Jr., *UFOs and Bible Prophecy* [Van Nuys, CA: Bible Voice, Inc., 1976], pp. 1–4).

During the next several days, Dr. Hymers learned more about Don. He discovered that Don had gone through the drug scene like so many young people today, had been jailed for dropping LSD in the water supply at a large political convention, and had come finally to San Francisco looking for answers to the tangled mess of his life. Doctor Hymers also discovered the root of Don's problems.

"Don had started on the road to insanity by reading a book . . . the *Urantia Book* . . . . It was this book that led Don into drugs, sexual perversion, and, finally, to jail. When he replaced this book with daily reading of the Bible, his mind began to clear. Through long prayer and counseling, I am glad to say, he has become a normal, productive human being . . . . Don had read a book reportedly written by men from outer space. He had become mentally deranged through it. Many would say he had become demonized. I have discovered this connection between the demonic and UFOs time and again" (Hymers, *UFOs and Bible Prophecy*, pp. 4, 5).

Similarities With Demons

Close Encounters of the Third Kind has been painstakingly based as closely as possible on actually UFO reports, many of them personally researched by Dr. J. Allen Hynek. Could it be that Roy Neary was acting out a mild form of demon possession? Could there have been a demon within him, causing him to lose his job, his wife and children—and almost his sanity? Did a demon urge him on toward Devil's Tower for the close encounter of the third kind?

Well, again, we must remind ourselves that *Close Encounters* is only a movie. Nonetheless, we must recognize, too, that Roy Neary was a *composite* person, whose experiences were based upon those recorded in actual, reported UFO encounters. How many people like the young man counseled by Dr. Hymers are being deceived at this very moment into believing the lies and deceptions of demons, while all the time believing they are hearing the truth from God?

Demons, according to the Bible, behave in ways which we see as being identical with the behavior of UFOnauts as reported by many contactees. Doctor Hymers writes: "In the Bible, demons predict the future (Acts 16:16); they project visions (Matthew 4:8); they pretend to be friendly and helpful while they really are out to destroy their victims (2 Corinthians 11:14); and they take various forms and shapes . . . . And each of these things is true of UFOs—they predict the future; they project visions; they pretend to be friendly, but really do their victims harm; and they take various forms" (Hymers, *UFOs and Bible Prophecy*, pp. 85, 86).

A Substitute for Christianity?

Author John Keel, a secular writer, tells how UFOs are deceiving people into the occult: "Flying saucers have given the pragmatists among us a substitute for the old-time religion. The new cultists speak of 'the evacuation,' when the great fleets of interplanetary spaceships will sweep down to gather up the chosen ones from the mountaintops and hustle them off to another planet just before earth explodes. We are reverting back to the age of the gods, once again. We may not be drilling holes in our heads, but several colleges and even some high schools are now offering courses in witchcraft, demonology, and flying saucers. While UFOs do terrify many witnesses, there are others who find confrontation with a glowing aerial mass to be an ecstatic, almost sexual experience. One woman recently told me about something that had happened

121

to her when she was a child. She and her parents had come across a great luminous sphere in a farm field and had watched in awe as it rose swiftly into the sky. For days afterwards her mother sat contentedly in a rocking chair on the front porch reliving the brief sighting and mumbling over and over, 'God loves me. God loves me'" (Keel, *The Eighth Tower*, p. 179).

Why Won't They Help Us?

Close Encounters of the Third Kind ends on the very upbeat note that UFOs are coming to help us in this troubled world, and to bring us salvation, immortality, and a better life in a better world somewhere out in space.

If this were really true of UFOs, then why do we read so many reports of evil, harmful behavior by UFOs? If UFOs are really here to help us, then what are they waiting for? Why haven't they made official contact and revealed their true purpose?

The only reasonable answer is that the UFO phenomenon is being caused by Satan and his demons. Their purpose is to confuse people about the true source of salvation, the Lord Jesus Christ. They want to create a church that is Christian in name only; in reality, it will be spiritually dead, controlled by Satan, and antichristian in doctrine and practice. Finally, UFOs are deception by demons preparing the world for Satan's evil dictator, the Antichrist, who will cause great and miraculous signs to be performed in order to deceive people into turning to himself in worship and away from Jesus Christ (*see* Revelation 13:13, 14).

Part 4
Encountering Immortality

10

When You Wish Upon a Star

Early in *Close Encounters of the Third Kind,* the Neary family was divided on whether to watch *The Ten Commandments* on TV, play "Goofey Golf," or go to the movies to see Walt Disney's, *Pinocchio.*

Roy Neary had seen the Disney classic several times as a boy, and now he wanted his kids to enjoy it, too. As he recalled the movie, he absentmindedly started to whistle its theme song: "When You Wish Upon a Star."

Unrealized Dreams

Roy always liked that song because it encouraged him, ignited a flame in his soul, for that hope that things were going to get better, that his own dreams would really come true. And Roy had plenty of dreams. Some were simply weird ideas, like auto-tennis, the electric toilet, and a worm ranch—all of which ended up in his basement. Then there were others, like his HO-model railroad that started out to be a once-in-a-while father-and-son pastime but which became an every weekend obsession for Roy.

Roy had had many dreams, all right, but, somehow, they just didn't pan out. Here he was, an ordinary hard hat, working for an ordinary employer—the Department of Water and Power—married to an ordinary wife, having ordinary kids, and living in an ordinary neighborhood. Make no mistake about it, though, Roy loved his wife and kids dearly. He liked his job, his home, his neighborhood—and especially the HO layout! But what had happened to all those dreams? And what about all those things he wanted to do, but just never found the time or money to do them?

Have you ever asked yourself, "Where have the years gone?" It's a question we often ponder starting from the time we graduate from adolescence. As youngsters, the immediate seems an adequate frame of time in which to accomplish all we want to do, while even a year seems like an eternity. Youth cannot wait to grow up, cannot wait for more time to pass, until a certain something hoped for comes into existence—such as a much anticipated Christmas Day, or later, the senior prom. To youth, time passes ever so slowly!

Each of us really has spent a great deal of time wishing upon stars, hoping that those precious desires in our hearts will come true—no matter how extreme!

A Life Too Short

As we get older, we begin to reflect on those dreams (the majority of which didn't come true—or at least not completely so). We start looking ahead and see that there are fewer and fewer years left in which to accomplish those goals and realize those dreams. As we grow older, time passes ever so fast!

In a land such as America, where there is so much opportunity, we easily recognize that there is enough challenge around us to take up the full span of *several* lifetimes, let alone only one. Indeed, how many times in a lifetime does a man switch careers just for the challenge and excitement of doing something new and different? How many mothers are taking off their aprons, only to replace them with laboratory smocks or even the workclothes of a phone-company technician?

How many marriages break up, just so a new life can be lived with a new mate? How many people don't even bother with the formality of a bona fide marriage because they know they will be moving on to someone else in time?

The question confronting young people today is not, *is* there a place for me? but rather, which road of opportunity shall I follow? Whichever it is, it must be flexible, and without long-term commitment.

Life is just too short to squeeze in all that we would like. Consequently, we feel that we fall short by a few years in our life span of attaining a satisfying position in life. Just when we acquire all the knowledge, amass the experience, make the contacts—have it all together—our bodies begin to wear out, and we are, all too soon, replaced by someone who is younger, someone with more mileage left!

The Appointed Life Span

We are told in the Bible that the appointed life span is one hundred twenty years (Genesis 6:3), though most of us wear out or conk out long before then. "Lord, make me to know my end," pleads the psalmist, "And what is the extent of my days, Let me know how transient I am" (Psalms 39:4 NAS).

Oh, how much easier it would be to plan our lives if we knew how much time we had left. Wouldn't the priorities change? Wouldn't we be more satisfied?

No, not really, unhappily. It wouldn't change anything in the end.

The psalmist shares the sobering truth: "For all our days have declined in Thy fury; We have finished our years like a sigh. As for the days of our life, they contain seventy years, Or if due to strength, eighty years, Yet their pride is but labor and sorrow; For soon it is gone and we fly away. Who understands the power of Thine anger, And Thy fury, according to the fear that is due Thee? So teach us to number our days, that we may present to Thee a heart of wisdom" (Psalms 90:9–12 NAS).

The truth is, we don't know how long we will live. "Why, you do not even know what will happen tomorrow. What is your life? You are a mist that appears for a little while and then vanishes" (James 4:14). ". . . All flesh is grass, and all its loveliness is like the flower of the field. The grass withers, the flower fades, When the breath of the Lord blows upon it; Surely the people are grass. The grass withers, the flower fades, but the word of our God stands forever" (Isaiah 40:6–8 NAS).

The Dream for a Better World

Roy Neary had reached the point in his life where he was beginning to wonder what life was all about. Is there any purpose, any sense to living? He had high hopes for a satisfied life. Happiness would come with marriage, and kids would bring even more happiness; and the job would really be fulfilling; and so would the autotennis and the HO railroad.

And so it goes across the country. We need a bigger house, a new car, fashionable clothes, a boat, a weekend cabin in the mountains.

Roy was ready to have his mind expanded. He had dreamed dreams of a new and better world, and now he was about to find it! At first, he didn't realize that the UFOnauts were communicating some sort of message to his brain. He didn't know that the strangely familiar shape he saw in the Rapid Shave or the mashed potatoes was familiar because the UFOnauts had planted the similarly shaped image of Devil's Tower in his mind. He was beckoned beyond Muncie, Indiana, and beyond this world, to Devil's Tower in Wyoming and a close encounter of the third kind that would lead him into the glorious new world he had dared to dream about and hope for.

While Roy Neary is not a real person and his story is not a real story, there is an element of truth in this particular aspect of the movie. Each of us has a little of Roy Neary in us. We dream about that bold new world, hoping that it will come—and with it, eternal satisfaction. Some of us learn the truth about this world, and others do not: There is nothing in this world that can truly satisfy us, and there is nothing in us that can find true satisfaction with anything in this world.

Finding Satisfaction

Yet, there is a way we can find satisfaction while we are in this world. For, just as Roy Neary was beckoned to Devil's Tower, we, too, hear a small voice that gives us a determination to live out our lives, to see this thing through, because it hints at a life beyond this one which is far greater. This is the promise of God being spoken to us in our hearts. It's written even more clearly in His Word, the Bible: "What profit is there to the worker from that in which he toils? I have seen the task which God has given the sons of men with which to occupy themselves. He has made everything appropriate in its time. He has also set eternity in their heart, yet so that man will not find out the work which God has done from the beginning even to the end. I know that there is nothing better for them than to rejoice and to do good in one's lifetime, moreover, that every man who eats and drinks sees good in all his labor—it is the gift of God" (Ecclesiastes 3:9–13 NAS).

"There is an appointed time for everything," we read a few verses earlier.

> There is an appointed time for everything. And there is a time for every event under heaven—
> A time to give birth, and a time to die;
> A time to plant, and a time to uproot what is planted.
> A time to kill, and a time to heal;
> A time to tear down, and a time to build up.
> A time to weep, and a time to laugh;
> A time to mourn, and a time to dance.
> A time to throw stones, and a time to gather stones;
> A time to embrace, and a time to shun embracing.

A time to search, and a time to give up as lost;
A time to keep, and a time to throw away.
A time to tear apart, and a time to sew together;
A time to be silent, and a time to speak.
A time to love, and a time to hate;
A time for war, and a time for peace.

Ecclesiastes 3:1–8 NAS

This means our life span—whether short or long—is adequate, that we have time to accomplish all that God wants us to accomplish. We need to remember that God has given us *exactly* enough time to do what He wants us to do. If we run out of time, then somewhere along the way, we stepped a bit outside of God's will for our lives.

God has given us purpose in life. And the reward we can look forward to for living according to His purpose is to spend eternity in a new and better world: "He has also set eternity in their heart." Instinctively, each of us *knows in our heart* that there is a life hereafter. God has placed that awareness within us! And, He has confirmed it through the revelation of His Word, the Bible, and His Son, Jesus Christ.

Without Eternity, Life Has No Purpose

If it weren't for this promise of eternal life and the knowledge that we have purpose in this lifetime, there would be no sense in anything in this life. Without God's guidance, without His promise of a life hereafter, it is " 'Vanity of vanities,' says the Preacher, 'Vanity of vanities! All is vanity.' What advantage does man have in all his work Which he does under the sun? A generation goes and a generation comes, But the earth remains forever . . . . I have seen all the works which have been done under the sun, and behold, all is vanity and striving after wind" (Ecclesiastes 1:2–4, 14 NAS).

". . . If the dead are not raised," the apostle Paul wrote to the Christians at Corinth, then, " 'Let us eat and drink, for tomorrow we die' " (1 Corinthians 15:32). Unhappily, the materialistic person indulges in eating and drinking—in all of the immediate and materialistic things of life. Such things as money, youth, and good health can bring only immediate satisfaction. But, when these are gone, what hope is there for the materialistic person to find satisfaction? For such a person the only solution to his dilemma is the dark voidness of death, beyond which he has no hope.

The Bible has much to say about the life beyond this worldly one. Yet, so many people look not to the Son of God for their passport to immortality but to vain religious sects, the occult, and the new space-age religions—even close encounters of the third kind with unidentified flying objects.

The apostle Peter said to Jesus: ". . . You have the words of eternal life. We believe and know that you are the Holy One of God" (John 6:68). On another occasion, Jesus proclaimed, "I am the way—and the truth and the life. No one comes to the Father except through me . . . Because I live, you also will live" (John 14:6, 19).

The song "When You Wish Upon a Star" tells us that anything our hearts desire will come to us. This song from *Pinocchio* is one of the most beautiful ever done for a motion picture. Yet, its theology is make-believe. Our wishes do not come true just because we might wish upon a star. Indeed, the desires of our heart come true when we are properly related to the one God of the universe, through His Son, the Lord Jesus Christ. There is a wonderful truth in the Book of Psalms, which reads:

Delight yourself in the Lord;
And He will give you the desires of your heart.
Commit your way to the Lord,
Trust also in Him, and He will do it.

Psalms 37:4, 5 NAS

11

The Evidence of Immortality

Close Encounters of the Third Kind started with the incredible discovery of a squadron of World War II planes that showed no apparent sign of wear or aging, although they had *disappeared three decades earlier!* But abruptly our attention was turned to other things, and we never again thought about the resurrected fighters until the film's climactic moments.

It was then that the mother spacecraft was setting down onto the landing pad, ever so slowly and gently. Below it the moog synthesizer was being used in an attempt to communicate with the occupants of the alien craft through the simple five-note tune and an accompanying array of rapidly changing colored lights on the giant "scoreboard" at the edge of the pad. The dazzling camera work and riveting musical score (heightened by Dolby Sound) made the whole affair a kind of psychedelic experience.

Finally, the cosmic sound-and-light-show ended. Claude Lacombe and the hundred or so technicians, scientists, and investigators who had witnessed the slow, methodical landing of the mother craft, now watched as the bottom of the ship slowly began to open. Strangely, the craft appeared more solid now than earlier when it seemed more semiphysical, perhaps pure light and energy. At first the observers saw a thin sliver of light shoot from the opening. But as the opening got bigger and bigger, the radiating beam of light broadened and became brighter and hotter as if they were gazing into the very depths of a giant furnace.

The extreme brightness was more than the men could stand. They turned away to protect their eyes. Some of them had dark glasses which they put on.

Once the bottom of the craft was fully opened and resting on the ground, the faint silhouettes of eight figures appeared in the cavity and began to emerge from the intense light and heat of the bowels of the craft. The bright light at first distorted the shapes, but as they came nearer, Lacombe and the others recognized them as—men!

Lacombe introduced himself to the men as they disembarked. They were young men, with dazed expressions on their faces. And they were dressed in naval flak jackets of the forties! These were the missing pilots. In all, more than two hundred dazed returnees disembarked the huge space carrier. One of the last of them was a tiny figure—that of three-year-old Barry Guiler!

Reunited With Loved Ones

Pushing and shoving her way past the throng of onlookers, Jillian cried out for Barry to come to her. The little fellow spotted his mother and gleefully ran into her waiting arms.

This tearful reunion ended a long ordeal which had begun so long ago and far away—back in Muncie, Indiana, when Barry was taken away by the UFO.

Other reunions were sure to follow, though the movie audience would never see them in the film. These were the reunions of the World War II pilots and others, with their families and friends from decades past. What was in store for the returnees?

What kind of reunions would they have? Can you visualize what it would be like to be reunited with a loved one you last saw more than thirty years ago? Wives in their fifties would be reunited with husbands who still looked like they did when they disappeared—in their twenties! Some of the pilots would even have children, grown, now, and the dads would appear even younger than their own sons and daughters!

We remind ourselves that *Close Encounters of the Third Kind* is only a fantasy movie. None of it really happened, although the movie's creators speculate that it *could*.

Is immortality a fanciful product dreamed up in Hollywood? Or is there such a thing? Can we somehow attain immortality?

The Reality of Immortality

Throughout the Old and New Testaments of the Bible are case histories of people whose experiences confirm the reality of immortality.

Enoch, who lived in the fortieth century before Christ, was taken up into heaven without having died (Genesis 5:24).

Another man, Elijah, who lived a thousand years before Christ, was, like Enoch, taken up by God into heaven. The Bible says that fifty-one people saw Elijah depart in a *fiery chariot!* (2 Kings 2:11). This wasn't a UFO, by the way, as some writers have suggested. Instead, it was a way of expressing in human terms the presence of God at the taking up of Elijah. Besides, how many cases have you heard reported about UFOs that looked like fiery chariots pulled by fiery horses?

The point, though, is this: If there were no

heaven—no life hereafter—God would not have taken Enoch and Elijah. Were there no heaven, God would have let them die. But God had other purposes for them—somewhere else. The taking up of Enoch and Elijah supports the existence of a life hereafter.

Then, there was Moses, the great leader of the ancient Hebrew people, who guided them out of bondage in Egypt some fifteen centuries before the birth of Christ. Centuries later, Jesus, along with His apostles, Peter, James, and John, went up on a high mountain, where the transfiguration of Jesus took place: "Just then there appeared before them Moses and Elijah, talking with Jesus" (Matthew 17:3). Where had Moses and Elijah been all those years? They had to have been somewhere! The deduction is obvious: They had been in the presence of God, in heaven; they had been enjoying a new kind of life in the hereafter. Again, the biblical record demonstrates the reality of life after the one we now live.

The Resurrection of Christ

No better example of resurrection into immortality exists than that of Jesus Christ. Even before His death, Jesus predicted that He would go to be with God in heaven: "There are many rooms in my Father's house . . . I am going there to prepare a place for you" (John 14:2).

Jesus died a physical death on the cross as well as a spiritual death (which is total separation from God). His spirit did not just vanish from existence, however, because we read in the Bible that He was quite active in another realm of existence: ". . . he went and preached to the spirits in prison [hell] who disobeyed long ago when God waited patiently in the days of Noah while the ark was being built . . ." (1 Peter 3:19, 20).

On the third day following His death at Calvary, Jesus rose from the dead. The apostle Paul summarized this wonderful event in a letter to the church at Corinth: ". . . Christ died for our sins according to the Scriptures, that he was buried, that he was raised on the third day according to the Scriptures, and that he appeared to Peter, and then to the Twelve [apostles]. After that, he appeared to more than five hundred of the brothers at the same time, most of whom are still living [so the story could have been verified by eyewitnesses] . . . . Then he appeared to James, then to all the apostles [again], and last of all he appeared to me also . . ." (1 Corinthians 15:3–8).

Remember the prediction Jesus made before His death that He would go to be with God in heaven and prepare a place there for His believers? Well, Jesus also promised then that He would come back for His believers: ". . . I will come back and take you to be with me that you also may be where I am" (John 14:3).

Then came the time for Jesus to be taken up into heaven. The apostle Luke recorded this in the Book of Acts: "After his suffering, he showed himself to these men [the apostles] and gave many convincing proofs that he was alive. He appeared to them over a period of forty days and spoke about the kingdom of God . . . . 'Lord,' [they asked,] 'are you at this time going to restore the kingdom to Israel?' He said to them: 'It is not for you to know the times or dates the Father has set by his own authority . . . ! After he said this, he was taken up before their very eyes, and a cloud hid him from their sight" (Acts 1:3, 6, 7, 9).

The apostles stood there, looking intently up into the sky as Jesus was drifting upward. Suddenly two men dressed in white stood beside them. " 'Men of Galilee,' they said, 'why do you stand here looking into the sky? This same Jesus, who has been taken from you into heaven, will come back in the same way you have seen him go into heaven' " (Acts 1:11).

In summary, then, the Resurrection of Christ proved the existence of the spiritual realm, because He had preached to the souls in hell between the time of His death and the time of His Resurrection. His Ascension into heaven and His prediction about going there to prepare a place for His believers further proved the existence of heaven as the place for the "born again" spirits of believers who die, physically. And, Christ's promise to return again proved that He fully intended on being in heaven for the intervening period of time.

Immortality and the Life Hereafter

The apostle Paul, in his first biblically recorded letter to his young disciple Timothy, makes it very clear that God "alone is immortal" (*see* 1 Timothy 6:16).

Does this mean that man is born with a body that is not immortal? It sure does. Just take a look at all the graveyards!

Ironically, man, in the beginning, *did* possess an immortal kind of body. Furthermore, man was spiritually related to God: there was no sin to separate man from fellowship with his Creator. But, as we discussed earlier, through Adam's sin, man's spiritual relationship with God was severed and, in this sense, all of Adam's descendents were condemned to spiritual death, too. Likewise, our bodies became mortal, having been immortal before sin. Now, they are subject to death.

But what about man's *spirit?* Well, it's important to realize that man's spirit does not become extinct at death. Instead, man's spirit either remains in a "dead" state (separated from God) or it is "born again" (reunited with God) by the believer's faith in Jesus Christ as Saviour and Lord. In this way a believer enters into eternal life, spiritually, at the exact moment he receives Christ as Saviour and Lord. ". . . you have been saved, through faith . . ." Paul wrote to the Christians at Ephesus (Ephesians 2:8).

Another apostle, John, wrote that all who believe already have eternal life: ". . . God has given us eternal life, and this life is in his Son. He who has the Son has life; he who does not have the Son of God does not have life. I write these things to you who believe in the name of the Son of God so that you may know that you have eternal life" (1 John 5:11–13). Notice that John didn't say, "you *will* have eternal life," or that "you *might* have eternal life." He said that all who believe in Christ already have eternal life, right now! "You *have* eternal life," he wrote, emphatically.

Death for the Unbeliever

So much for the believer in Christ. Now, what happens to the *unbeliever* when he or she passes from this life into death?

Jesus answered this question by giving the illustration of the true experience of a rich man and a

141

poor man named Lazarus. When the time came for both men to die, poor Lazarus went to be with the Hebrew patriarch, Abraham, in heaven, and the rich man went to be in hell.

" 'In hell, where he [the rich man] was in torment, he looked up and saw Abraham far away, with Lazarus by his side. So he called to him, "Father Abraham, have pity on me and send Lazarus to dip the tip of his finger in water and cool my tongue, because I am in agony in this fire." But Abraham replied, "Son, remember that in your lifetime you received your good things, while Lazarus received bad things, but now he is comforted here and you are in agony" ' " (Luke 16:23–25).

While the body of this rich man eventually turned into dust in the grave, just as Adam's did and all who had died since then, the rich man's spirit went to be in hell. This example shows that the spirits of unbelievers will suffer for their wickedness (vv. 23, 24), will be fully conscious of what is happening in hell as well as in heaven (vv. 23, 24), and will be in complete possession of their memories (v. 25).

" ' "And besides all this, [said Abraham to the rich man] between us and you a great chasm has been fixed, so that those who want to go from here to you cannot, nor can anyone cross over from there to us" ' " (Luke 16:26). This passage explains the horrible truth that once an unbeliever dies and goes to hell, he will be out of reach of any possible attempt by others to comfort him and will remain in the place of torment forever, without chance of escape.

Man personally must bear the terrible consequences for not listening to the warnings of Scripture. Jesus' story about Lazarus and the rich man concludes with this chilling warning: The rich man said to Abraham: " ' "I beg you, father, send Lazarus to my father's house, for I have five brothers. Let him warn them, so that they will not also come to this place of torment." Abraham replied, "They have Moses and the Prophets; let them listen to them." "No, father Abraham," he said, "but if someone from the dead goes to them, they will repent." He said to him, "If they do not listen to Moses and the Prophets, they will not be convinced even if someone rises from the dead" ' " (Luke 16:27–31).

Death for the Believer

The Bible gives the believer a hope that the unbeliever does not have. Immediately upon death, the spirit of the believer goes to be with Jesus Christ (Philippians 1:23) and his body, though it turns to dust like the one of the unbeliever who dies, will be resurrected into an immortal body at the return of Jesus Christ.

Jesus taught that, " '. . . unless a man is born again, he cannot see the kingdom of God . . . . For God so loved the world that he gave his one and only Son, that whoever believes in him shall not perish but have everlasting life' " (John 3:3, 16).

" 'I tell you the truth [said Jesus], whoever hears my word and believes him who sent me has eternal life and will not be condemned; he has crossed over from death to life' " (John 5:24). Even though a believer is still alive in this world, in this mortal body, he *has* eternal life," Jesus said. Such a believer has already "crossed over from death to life," Jesus explained.

Though a believer must still die a physical death, God promises that a believing man's mortal body will be resurrected to receive immortality at the time of Christ's second coming.

This truth was taught by the apostle Paul and explained in a letter to the church at Corinth:

I declare to you, brothers, that flesh and blood cannot inherit the kingdom of God, nor does the perishable inherit the imperishable. Listen, I tell you a mystery: We shall not all sleep, but we shall all be changed—in a flash, in the twinkling of an eye, at the last trumpet. For the trumpet will sound, the dead will be raised imperishable, and we shall be changed. For the perishable must clothe itself with the imperishable, and the mortal with immortality.

1 Corinthians 15:50–53

Immortality for the believer is spoken of by Jesus on numerous occasions, according to the record of Scripture: " '. . . if a man keeps my word, he will never see death . . . . I give them eternal life, and they shall never perish; no one can snatch them out of my hand . . . . I am the resurrection and the life. He who believes in me will live, even though he dies; and whoever lives and believes in me will never die . . .' " (John 8:51; 10:28; 11:25, 26).

The Bible also tells about a second resurrection. Christ will return to earth and reign for one thousand years. After that, there will be a second resurrection of all dead unbelievers who will have died from since the beginning of mankind. These resurrected unbelievers will be judged and, because they are sinners, will be found guilty. They will be sentenced to the "second death," which is eternal hell (Revelation 20).

Hell is the place of everlasting torment. It is the horrible fate of all who remain spiritually dead because they refuse to believe in Jesus Christ as Lord, and to receive His forgiveness of their sins and His free gift of salvation.

Victory Over Death

This second death has no power over the believer because in this present life he or she trusts Christ and has received forgiveness of sins and the gift of eternal life (Revelation 20:6).

The apostle Paul explained this wonderful miracle in the lives of all who believed:

> When the perishable has been clothed with the imperishable, and the mortal with immortality, then the saying that is written will come true: "Death has been swallowed up in victory."
> "Where, O death is your victory?
> Where, O death, is your sting?"
> The sting of death is sin, and the power of sin is the law. But thanks to God! He gave us the victory through our Lord Jesus Christ.
>
> 1 Corinthians 15:54–57

Believers can have the confidence of knowing that Jesus defeated death when He rose from the grave, and ". . . the one who raised the Lord Jesus from the dead will also raise us. . ." (2 Corinthians 4:14).

Since the bodies of believers are but flesh and blood, Jesus shared in their humanity, ". . . so that by his death he might destroy him who holds the power of death—that is, the devil—and free those who all their lives were held in slavery by their fear of death" (Hebrews 2:14, 15).

Jesus Christ ". . . has destroyed death and has brought life and immortality to light through the gospel" (2 Timothy 1:10).

Part 5
Encountering the Infinite Kind

12

Close Encounter of the Infinite Kind

Roy Neary was lonesome. Sure, he had a wife and kids—and he loved them dearly. But, still, he was lonesome. Something was missing in his life. He couldn't put his finger on it, but something was definitely missing.

When the UFO invasion began, Roy somehow *knew* that the strange longing he had was about to end. That missing *something* in his life was about to be found. It was on the horizon, beckoning him onward. His lonesome heart was searching, questioning. Soon it would be satisfied. It would find its peace, discover the mystifying answers that had always eluded him. This was the hope Roy had. It began like a tiny spark, but then, it ignited his soul. The dreams he had dared to dream and the hopes he had ventured to hope were about to come true.

Irresistibly drawn to Devil's Tower, his lonesome journey through life had come to its end. A new life was about to begin—a life of belonging, understanding, and purpose.

The Movie People Have Waited For

Movie critic, Ray Bradbury, expressed his interpretation this way: *"Close Encounters of the Third Kind* is the science-fiction film we have all been waiting for. In fact, we were waiting for it before we were born. The ghost in us, the secret stuff of genetics, was waiting. The Life Force was waiting, waiting to be born, waiting to be called forth.

"Close Encounters calls. We feel ourselves being born, truly, for the first time . . . . This is a religious film . . . . We have need to be bound together to the universe, the cosmos. We have needed to collect our souls . . . . We are, after all, the Star Children . . . . *Close Encounters* knows exactly where the center of the universe is . . . . And the center is that moment in Time when two fleshes reach across a five billion year experiment in birthing and look upon each other. . . ." (Ray Bradbury, *Los Angeles Times,* November 20, 1977.)

Space-Age Religion

Steven Spielberg, Ray Bradbury, Erich von Daniken, and Josef Blumrich, along with so many others, have become the oracles of our times. They have felt the pulse of a hurting world and diagnosed the illness as terminal. But they hold out hope that an extraterrestrial saviour is on his way. If only the world can hold on—survive—until he arrives!

Spielberg would have us believe this space-age religion and accept its speculative new gospel as the truth.

The prophets of the new space-age religion would have us believe that man, through his own brand of religion, can encounter the infinite power of the universe and become a "star child" in some immortal sense.

Incredibly, people are so hungry to know the infinite God—and yet so spiritually blind to the truth—that they fabricate their own speculative religions in hope that they might encounter God. Gone are the days of shaping religious idols out of clay, wood, or gold, and here is the day of creating idols and vain religions through motion pictures, television, books, and the like.

Saul's Close Encounter

With so many conflicting gospels being proclaimed in the world today, just what is a person to believe?

The apostle Paul encountered a similar dilemma nearly two thousand years ago, in the city of Galatia, where the Christians there were being confused by the infiltrating false gospels. Paul wrote to them:

> I am astonished that you are so quickly deserting the one who called you by the grace of Christ and are turning to a different gospel—which is really no gospel at all. Evidently some people are throwing you into confusion and are trying to pervert the gospel of Christ. But even if we or an angel from heaven should preach a gospel other than the one we preached to you, let him be eternally condemned! . . . the gospel I preached is not something that man made up. I did not receive it from any man, nor was I taught it; rather, I received it by revelation from Jesus Christ.
>
> Galatians 1:6–8, 11, 12

Paul had been born of Jewish parents and was a Roman citizen by virtue of his birth in Tarsus. Called Saul of Tarsus in his early years, he had ". . . violently persecuted the church of God and tried to destroy it" (Galatians 1:13). He was advancing in Judaism beyond many Jews of his own age and was extremely zealous in his religious practices. But then Paul had a close encounter of the infinite kind—with Jesus Christ. It happened on the road to Damascus when Paul was setting out to capture Christians and return them to Jerusalem as prisoners.

As he neared Damascus on his journey, suddenly a light from heaven flashed around him. He fell to the ground and heard a voice say to him, "Saul, Saul, why do you persecute me?"

"Who are you, Lord?" Saul asked.

"I am Jesus whom you are persecuting," he replied. "Now get up and go into the city, and you will be told what you must do."

Acts 9:3–6

Several men were traveling with Saul. They stood there speechless because they had heard the voice of Christ but had seen nothing.

Saul got up from the ground, but when he opened his eyes he could see nothing. So they led him by the hand into Damascus. For three days he was blind, and did not eat or drink anything.

Acts 9:8, 9

Meanwhile, in Damascus, a disciple named Ananias experienced a vision in which he heard the voice of Christ:

"Go to the house of Judas on Straight Street and ask for a man from Tarsus named Saul, for he is praying. In a vision he has seen a man named Ananias come and place his hands on him to restore his sight."

"Lord," Ananias answered, "I have heard many reports about this man and all the harm he has done to your saints in Jerusalem. And he has come here with authority from the chief priest to arrest all who call on your name."

But the Lord said to Ananias, "Go! This man is my chosen instrument to carry my name before the Gentiles and their kings and before the people of Israel. I will show him how much he must suffer for my name."

Then Ananias went to the house and entered it. Placing his hands on Saul, he said, "Brother Saul, the Lord—Jesus, who appeared to you on the road as you were coming here—has sent me so that you may see again and be filled with the Holy Spirit." Immediately, something like scales fell from Saul's eyes, and he could see again . . . .

Saul spent several days with the disciples in Damascus. At once he began to preach in the synagogues that Jesus is the Son of God. All those who heard him were astonished and asked, "Isn't he the man who raised havoc in Jerusalem among those who call on this name? And hasn't he come here to take them as prisoners to the chief priests?" Yet Saul grew more and more powerful and baffled the Jews living in Damascus by proving that Jesus is the Christ.

After many days had gone by, the Jews conspired to kill him, but Saul learned of their plan. Day and night they kept close watch on the city gates in order to kill him. But his followers took him by night and lowered him in a basket through an opening in the wall.

When he came to Jerusalem, he tried to join the disciples, but they were all afraid of him, not believing that he really was a disciple. But Barnabas took him and brought him to the apostles. He told them how Saul on his journey had seen the Lord and that the Lord had spoken to him, and how in Damascus he had preached fearlessly in the name of Jesus. So Saul stayed with them and moved about freely in Jerusalem, speaking boldly in the name of the Lord. He talked and debated with the Grecian Jews, but they tried to kill him. When the brothers learned of this, they took him down to Caesarea and sent him off to Tarsus.

Acts 9:11–18, 20–30

The apostle Paul was but one of many men who experienced life-changing encounters with Jesus some two thousand years ago.

Encountering the "Lamb of God"

John the Baptist was a man of the wilderness who dressed in clothes made of coarse camel's hair and ate locusts and wild honey. He had been traveling throughout the countryside, proclaiming that the Kingdom of God was at hand, and baptizing people in water for repentance of their sins. Then Jesus approached John one day, and was baptized, though

154

He Himself had never or would never commit a single sin.

" 'Look,' " said John the Baptist, " 'the Lamb of God, who takes away the sin of the world!' " (John 1:29). Then John baptized Jesus. " 'I saw the Spirit come down from heaven as a dove and remain on him,' " John testified. " 'I would not have known him, except that the one who sent me to baptize with water told me, "The man on whom you see the Spirit come down and remain is he who will baptize with the Holy Spirit." I have seen and I testify that this is the Son of God' " (John 1:32).

Fishers of Men

Not long afterward, two brothers—Peter and Andrew—who were fishermen, encountered Jesus. He approached them as they were casting a net into the lake. " 'Come, follow me,' Jesus said, 'and I will make you fishers of men.' At once they left their nets and followed him" (Matthew 4:19, 20).

What was it about this man Jesus that would cause fishermen to drop their nets and follow Him, no questions asked, leaving behind them their jobs, material possessions, friends and family? It was because they recognized Him as the Messiah (which in Greek is translated *Christ*) whose coming had been foretold in the Scriptures by the ancient Hebrew prophets.

More disciples joined the throng, including Nathanael, who said to Jesus, " '. . . you are the Son of God; you are the King of Israel' " (John 1:49).

The Bible tells us that, "Jesus went throughout Galilee teaching in their synagogues, preaching the good news of the kingdom, and healing every disease and sickness among the people. News about

155

him spread all over Syria, and people brought to him all who were ill with various diseases, those suffering severe pain, the demon-possessed, the epileptics and the paralytics, and he healed them. Large crowds from Galilee, the Decapolis, Jerusalem, Judea and the region across the Jordan followed him" (Matthew 4:23–25).

Jesus demonstrated that He was the Son of God in other ways, as well, such as controlling nature and the elements. When a furious storm came up on the lake, threatening to capsize the boat in which Jesus and His disciples were sailing, they woke Him, pleading, " 'Lord, save us! We're going to drown!'

"He replied, 'You of little faith, why are you so afraid?' Then he got up and rebuked the winds and the waves, and it was completely calm.

"The men were amazed and asked, 'What kind of man is this? Even the winds and the waves obey him!' " (Matthew 8:25–27).

Another time Jesus took five loaves of bread and two fishes and, giving thanks to His Father in heaven, supernaturally multiplied them so that they satisfied the hunger of five thousand people! Afterward, His disciples collected twelve basketfuls of scraps from the feast (Matthew 14:13–21).

Encountering the Almighty

Not long before His crucifixion, Jesus took the disciples, Peter, James, and John up on a high mountain. There, the men saw the transfiguration of Jesus which their eyes could hardly believe. "His face shone like the sun, and his clothes became as white as the light" (Matthew 17:2). As if that were not enough, there appeared before them two men who had walked the earth generations and genera-

156

tions before them—Moses and Elijah! At that moment, ". . . a bright cloud enveloped them, and a voice from the cloud said, 'This is my Son, whom I love; with him I am well-pleased. Listen to him!'

"When the disciples heard this, they fell face down to the ground, terrified. But Jesus came and touched them. 'Get up,' He said. 'Don't be afraid.' When they looked up, they saw no one except Jesus.

"As they were coming down the mountain, Jesus instructed them, 'Don't tell anyone what you have seen, until the Son of Man has been raised from the dead' " (Matthew 17:5–9).

The Giver of Life

There was a man named Lazarus, who became sick and then died. Jesus went to comfort the man's sisters, Mary and Martha. Martha believed that if Jesus had come earlier, He might have healed her brother, Lazarus, and that he would still be alive.

Jesus was deeply moved by Martha's faith. He asked to be taken to the tomb of Lazarus, which was a cave. Outside, a crowd of people gathered to see what Jesus would do.

"Take away the stone," he said.

"But, Lord," said Martha, the sister of the dead man, "by this time there is a bad odor, for he has been there four days."

Then Jesus said, "Did I not tell you that if you believed, you would see the glory of God?"

So they took away the stone. Then Jesus looked up and said, "Father, I thank you that you have heard me. I knew that you always hear me, but I said this for the benefit of the people standing here, that they may believe that you sent me."

When he had said this, Jesus called in a loud voice, "Lazarus, come out!" The dead man came out, his hands and feet wrapped with strips of linen, and a cloth around his face.

Jesus said to them, "Take off the grave clothes and let him go."

John 11:39–44

Encounter at Calvary

Jesus shocked His apostles by predicting that one of His own would soon betray Him. Not long afterward, His prediction came true. Judas Iscariot, one of the twelve, conspired with the Jewish priesthood for the arrest of Christ. In short order, Jesus was seized, quickly tried, and sentenced to be crucified at a place called The Skull. Two other men, both of them criminals, were crucified with Him, one on His left and the other on His right.

The people stood watching, and the rulers even sneered at him. They said, "He saved others; let him save himself if he is the Christ of God, the Chosen One."

The soldiers also came up and mocked him. They offered him wine vinegar and said, "If you are the king of the Jews, save yourself."

There was a written notice above him, which read: THIS IS THE KING OF THE JEWS.

One of the criminals who hung there hurled insults at him: "Aren't you the Christ? Save yourself and us!"

But the other criminal rebuked him. "Don't you fear God," he said, "since you are under the same sentence? We are punished justly, for we are getting what our deeds deserve. But this man has done nothing wrong."

Then he said, "Jesus, remember me when you come into your kingdom."

Jesus answered him, "I tell you the truth, today you will be with me in paradise."

Luke 23:35–43

One thief rejected Christ, the other believed in Him. One would spend eternity in hell, and the other in heavenly paradise with Jesus.

The hours went by, and Jesus hung there on the cross, praying for His tormentors, " 'Father, forgive them, for they do not know what they are doing' " (Luke 23:34). He suffered insults and cruel treatment. Then, by the ninth hour (from sunrise, until three o'clock in the afternoon), the sun supernaturally stopped shining, and the sky became dark. (It couldn't have been an eclipse, because there was a full Passover moon.) At the same hour, another strange event took place: the curtain of the temple was torn. This curtain, which was made of such heavy material that a man could not have torn it, separated the Holy Place, where the priests ministered, from the presence of God in the Holy of Holies. This, too, was a distinctly supernatural act.

It was at this precise moment that Jesus cried out in a loud voice from the cross: " 'Father, into your hands I commit my spirit.' When he had said this, he breathed his last" (Luke 23:46).

Encountering the Empty Tomb

The body of Jesus was removed from the cross and placed in a tomb carved out of rock. Three days later, on Sunday morning, the women who had

come with Jesus from Galilee, took spices and per-
fumes to the tomb. But when they arrived, they
found the stone, which had sealed the entrance, had
been rolled away. They entered the tomb and did
not find the body of the Lord Jesus.

While they were wondering about this, suddenly two men in clothes that gleamed like
lightning stood beside them. In their fright the
women bowed down with their faces to the
ground, but the men said to them, "Why do you
look for the living among the dead? He is not
here; he has risen! Remember how he told you,
while he was still with you in Galilee: 'The Son
of Man must be delivered into the hands of sinful men, be crucified and on the third day be
raised again.'" Then they remembered His
words.

Luke 24:4–8

The women returned from the empty tomb and
told all these things to the apostles and to all the
others. Their story was dismissed as nonsense by
nearly everyone—all except for the apostle Peter.
Remembering the words of the Lord, he excitedly
ran to the tomb, where he found only the strips of
burial linen that had covered the body of Jesus. But
the body was nowhere to be found.

Later that same day, two of the apostles were
going to a village called Emmaus, which is located
about seven miles from Jerusalem. As they walked
along the dusty road, discussing the things which
had happened that day, ". . . Jesus himself came
up and walked along with them; but they were kept
from recognizing him.

"He asked them, 'What are you discussing together as you walk along?' " (Luke 24: 15, 16).

They then told Him everything they knew about the events of the past three days—the crucifixion, the empty tomb.

Jesus accompanied the two into the village where He accepted their invitation to join them for dinner. "When he was at the table with them, he took bread, gave thanks, broke it and began to give it to them. Then their eyes were opened and they recognized him, and he disappeared from their sight . . . . They got up and returned at once to Jerusalem. There they found the Eleven and those with them, assembled together and saying, 'It is true! The Lord has risen and has appeared to Simon.' Then the two told what had happened on the way, and how Jesus was recognized by them when he broke the bread" (Luke 24:30, 31, 33–35).

That evening, all the apostles were together, behind locked doors for fear of the Jews. Suddenly, Jesus came and appeared among them, saying, ". . . 'Peace be with you.' " (Luke 24:36). Then He showed them the nail marks on His hands and His side. You can imagine their joy in seeing their resurrected Saviour and Lord!

Thomas wasn't there, however, and when the others told him what had happened, he said he wouldn't believe it unless he could see the nail marks in His hands and put his finger where the nails were, and put his hand into His wounded side. A week later Thomas got his chance. The apostles were together—Thomas included, this time—and Jesus came and stood among them. " 'Put your finger here; see my hands,' " Jesus said to Thomas. " 'Reach out your hand and put it into my side.

161

Stop doubting and believe.'

"Thomas said to him, 'My Lord and my God!' " (John 20:26–28).

Then the apostles encountered the risen Christ a third time. It happened when they were fishing by the Sea of Tiberias. They fished all night, but without catching any fish. Morning came, and Jesus stood on the shore, unrecognized by His apostles. He told them to throw their net out on the right side of the boat, which they did, and were unable to haul the net back in because it quickly filled with so many fish! Then the apostles recognized the figure on the shore as Jesus. They went to Him and enjoyed breakfast together (John 21:1–14).

After that, Jesus appeared to more than five hundred Christians at the same time, and then to James, one of the apostles (1 Corinthians 15:6, 7). He appeared again to the apostles at the time of His Ascension into heaven: ". . . he was taken up before their very eyes, and a cloud hid him from their sight.

"They were looking intently up into the sky as he was going, when suddenly two men dressed in white stood beside them. 'Men of Galilee,' they said, 'why do you stand here looking into the sky? This same Jesus, who has been taken from you into heaven, will come back in the same way you have seen him go into heaven' " (Acts 1:9–11).

A Personal Encounter

Many of the people who lived at the time of Jesus had the privilege of knowing Him personally, seeing Him, and hearing Him teach God's truth. Even so, one thief at Calvary rejected Him, while the other believed. The chief priests and members of the Sanhedrin encountered Jesus Christ, too, but few of them believed in Him. Even Thomas, one of the Lord's own apostles, doubted that his brothers had seen their resurrected Master, and he had to encounter the risen Christ face to face before he would believe He had risen from the grave.

After Christ's Ascension into heaven, people continued to encounter Him—by faith, through the teaching of His apostles and the Scriptures. Even now, in the twentieth century, men and women, boys and girls—the educated and the illiterate, the rich and the poor—are encountering Jesus Christ in a personal way. These are the ones who have become spiritually "born again," just as Jesus had explained to Nicodemus (John 3).

A recent Gallup poll reveals that more than fifty million adult Americans claim to be born-again Christians. And there are another twenty-five million under eighteen years of age! Among these believers are such notables as President Jimmy Carter; Watergate figure Charles Colson; Pat Boone; Norma Zimmer; cowboy actor Ty Hardin; the "Galloping Gourmet," Graham Kerr; and the list goes on and on.

Many people believe that in this generation all the nations of the world will have the opportunity to encounter Jesus Christ. Indeed, Jesus told His disciples, " 'All authority in heaven and on earth has been given to me. Therefore go and make disciples of all nations, baptizing them in the name of the Father and of the Son and of the Holy Spirit, and teaching them to obey everything I have commanded you. And surely I will be with you always, to the very end of the age' " (Matthew 28:18–20).

Now Jesus Christ would never command His followers to do anything He wouldn't give them the power to accomplish—power through His Holy Spirit. The apostle Matthew recorded the prophecy given by Jesus that " 'this gospel of the kingdom will be preached in the whole world as a testimony to all nations, and then the end will come' " (Matthew 24:14). When that is accomplished, when the entire world has heard the good news of Jesus Christ, then Jesus will return. Those who encountered Him and *rejected* Him will be judged and found guilty. Those who encountered Him and *received* Him as their personal Saviour and Lord will be rewarded and will spend eternity in the presence of God. Theirs truly will be a close encounter of the infinite kind.

13

Signs in the Skies

Dusk finally had fallen, and Roy and Jillian sat perched on the rocky slope of Devil's Tower. They were safe, for the moment, at least, from the army helicopter's paralyzing nerve dust. But now something different was happening in the sky over Devil's Tower.

On the floor of the landing pad below, a technician reported to Lacombe that targets were showing up on radar. Then the men began looking skyward and pointing up. Roy and Jillian looked up, too, and saw it.

High cumulus clouds were rapidly moving toward Devil's Tower. Churning and boiling, the clouds mushroomed larger and larger. Then an electrical storm erupted within the turbulent mass. It was a fantastic sight—bursts of light flashed through the clouds like a gigantic fireworks display.

The celestial light show terrified Jillian, reminding her of the frightening day Barry was taken.

In moments the lights skyrocketed out of the clouds. They were back! The UFO invasion had begun! The extraterrestrials were preparing to land, and Roy, Jillian, and Lacombe and his team were about to experience a close encounter of the third kind!

Everyone was thrilled by this fantastic experience. It was far beyond their wildest fantasies, like being in a dream. Many of them could only stare in childlike wonderment at the spectacle unfolding before them. Several of Lacombe's technicians became oblivious to the jobs they were supposed to be doing, and just stood there, staring with innocent, wide-eyed enchantment.

The Second Coming

The strange cloud formations over Devil's Tower, the spectacle of the UFO invasion, the aliens, the missing navy pilots, the choosing of Roy and the others for a journey aboard the mother craft—these events combine in *Close Encounters* to create a happening that parallels in many ways those things which will take place at the second coming of Jesus Christ. Indeed, the response of Roy, Lacombe, and the others to what was happening was no less than if they actually had been witnessing the second coming of Christ!

Jesus told His apostles that He would return at the end of the age, after a time characterized by these signs: imposters who claim to be Christ, wars and rumors of wars, famines, earthquakes, persecution, martyrdom, unspiritual behavior among believers, betrayal, hatred, and false prophets. The entire account of what Jesus predicted is recorded in Matthew 24. Many of these conditions are seen in the world today. They will increase and intensify as history nears that momentous time of the return of Christ.

"For then there will be great tribulation," Jesus prophesied, "such as has not occurred since the beginning of the world until now, nor ever shall" (Matthew 24:21 NAS).

The world will be racked by widespread lawlessness. Believers will be severely persecuted at the hands of the Antichrist—Satan's ambassador from hell. Few people will remain who love God.

According to the prophet Daniel, seven years before the return of Christ, the Antichrist will sign a peace treaty in the Middle East, between Israel and her neighbors (Daniel 9:27). The first three and a half years will be relatively peaceful; however, midpoint of the period, the Antichrist will impose emperor worship on everyone, killing all who do not bow down to him (*see* 2 Thessalonians 2; Revelation 13). (*See also* Frank Allnutt, *Antichrist: After the Omen* [Old Tappan, NJ: Fleming H. Revell Co., 1977].)

Like Ezekiel's Cloud

The boiling, erupting clouds seen by Roy and Jillian were the means by which the UFOs revealed themselves and ultimately made contact with people on earth. Correspondingly, God revealed Himself in clouds on many occasions in the Old Testament, and the Ascension of Christ and His return are cloud related, according to the New Testament.

The prophet Ezekiel describes a vision through which God came to him in the clouds: "And as I looked, behold, a storm wind was coming from the north, a great cloud with fire flashing forth continually and a bright light around it, and in its midst something like glowing metal in the midst of the fire" (Ezekiel 1:4 NAS).

As we discussed earlier, what Ezekiel had seen in this vision was the presence of God, symbolized by a cloud, burning and flashing with light in a way that made it resemble a glowing, burning metallic object.

167

Clouds are common biblical expressions for the presence of God. There are many more examples. One is when Moses led the people of Israel out of bondage in Egypt: "And the Lord was going before them in a pillar of cloud by day to lead them on the way, and in a pillar of fire by night to give them light, that they might travel by day and by night" (Exodus 13:21 NAS).

Later, in the Book of Exodus, we read that God instructed Moses to set up a tent for worship. When Moses completed the task, "Then the cloud covered the tent of meeting, and the glory of the Lord filled the tabernacle" (Exodus 40:34 NAS). Again and again, the Bible demonstrates God's presence as being associated with or symbolized by clouds.

Ascending in a Cloud

The apostle Luke writes in the Book of Acts that forty days after the Resurrection of Christ, He told His apostles to wait in Jerusalem for the coming of the Holy Spirit. Then, "After he said this, he was taken up before their very eyes, and a cloud hid him from their sight" (Acts 1:9).

Certainly, Jesus could command clouds to behave in such a way, just as He could calm the seas. Obviously, He didn't need the help of a mechanical vehicle—a UFO, as some suggest—to transport Him. Regardless, the question is justifiably raised, "Was it an ordinary cloud?"

According to Dr. George E. Ladd, "the cloud was probably not a cloud of vapor but the cloud of glory signalizing the divine presence. At His transfiguration Jesus had entered the cloud of the divine presence but did not remain there. At the ascension He enters it again and remains with the Father"

168

(George E. Ladd, *A Theology of the New Testament*
[Grand Rapids: Eerdmans, 1974], p. 334).

Signs in the Skies

Just as the turbulent, flashing clouds seen in
Close Encounters announced the coming of the
UFO invasion, with its godlike alien beings, so too
will signs in the skies signal the second coming of
Jesus Christ. Approximately seven years after the
Antichrist's Middle East peace treaty is signed,
Jesus will return, according to His own prophesies:

" 'Immediately after the distress of those days,' "
Jesus pointed out, quoting from the prophecy of
Isaiah, " ' "the sun will be darkened, and the moon
will not give its light; the stars will fall from the sky,
and the heavenly bodies will be shaken."

" 'At that time the sign of the Son of Man will
appear in the sky, and all the nations of the earth
will mourn. They will see the Son of Man *coming
on the clouds* of the sky, with power and great
glory' " (Matthew 24:29, 30, italics added).

What an incredibly joyous, wonderfully awesome
spectacle it will be for believers when this happens!
The clouds will behave in such a way as to unmis-
takably indicate that the second coming of Christ is
at hand!

The return of Christ in the clouds has been anticipated by believers for centuries. The apostle
Luke recorded the words of the two angelic beings
who spoke to the apostles at the time of Christ's
Ascension in a cloud into heaven: " 'Men of Galilee,
why do you stand looking into the sky? This Jesus,
who has been taken up from you into heaven, will
come in just the same way as you have watched Him
go into heaven' " (Acts 1:11 NAS). The prophet

Daniel wrote that the Son of Man would come with the clouds of heaven (Daniel 7:13). And the apostle Paul wrote that Jesus will return in the clouds (1 Thessalonians 4:17).

Cosmic Communications

The medium of communication in *Close Encounters* between the visitors from outer space and men on earth was music. The simple five notes were heard early in the film, only to become transformed into symphony-orchestra-supported solos by a tuba and an oboe at the time of the climactic encounter. This music was used by the aliens to get the attention of the people on earth, to announce their coming.

When Jesus Christ returns, there will be audible signs announcing His coming. The apostle Paul writes that the voice of the archangel Michael will be heard (1 Thessalonians 4:16; cf. Daniel 12:1; Jude 9). And, Jesus will give a shout that will be heard around the world, not only by the living (Revelation 18:4), but also by dead believers (Revelation 11:12).

Multitudes of believers from throughout the world and from all of history will join angelic beings before the returned Christ and praise Him in unison (Revelation 7:10–12; 11:17, 18). A multitude of 144,000 "who had been redeemed from the earth" will sing praises to Christ (Revelation 14:3). Those who had been victorious over the beast (Revelation 15:2) will sing as well.

Close Encounters had tuba and oboe solos to announce the arrival of the godlike aliens. The Bible tells us that the return of Jesus Christ will be heralded by the sounding of the last *trumpet:* "And the seventh angel sounded (a trumpet); and there arose loud voices in heaven, saying, 'The kingdom of the world has become the kingdom of our Lord, and of His Christ; and He will reign forever and ever' " (Revelation 11:15 NAS). This prophecy of the last trumpet is mentioned also in Matthew 24:31; 1 Corinthians 15:52; 1 Thessalonians 4:16.

The Chief Alien

Three distinct kinds of beings emerged from the mother craft in *Close Encounters,* including the chief alien (who some have likened to the dough boy seen on Pillsbury's TV commercials). When Jesus Christ returns, He will be accompanied by the archangel Michael and the angels of heaven: "The armies of heaven were following him, riding on white horses and dressed in fine linen, white and clean" (Revelation 19:14).

Return of the Navy Pilots

As the World War II navy pilots wandered in a daze out of the incredible brightness of the mother craft's interior, it immediately became apparent to the astonished technicians that the airmen appeared not to have aged since they had disappeared three decades earlier! When Christ returns, all of history's departed believers will be raised from the dead and given new, immortal bodies. Think about this for a moment! It means they will never die, or be susceptible to injury or sickness. These bodies will be like the glorified body of Christ, which means they will be totally immune to sin. This will make them suitable to be in the holy presence of God (Ephesians 2:1–3; Philippians 3:20, 21).

The apostle Paul writes about this wonderful mystery in several of his letters:

Listen, I tell you a mystery: We shall not all sleep, but we shall all be changed—in a flash, in the twinkling of an eye, at the last trumpet. For the trumpet will sound, the dead will be raised imperishable, and we shall be changed.
1 Corinthians 15:51, 52

Brothers, we do not want you to be ignorant about those who sleep, or to grieve like the rest of men, who have no hope. We believe that Jesus died and rose again and so we believe that God will bring with Jesus those who sleep in him. According to the Lord's own word, we tell you that we who are still alive, who are left till the coming of the Lord, will certainly not precede those who have fallen asleep. For the Lord himself will come down from heaven, with a loud command, with the voice of the archangel and with the trumpet call of God, and the dead in Christ will rise first."
1 Thessalonians 4:13–16

" 'Do not be amazed at this,' " said Jesus, " 'for a time is coming when all who are in their graves will hear his voice and come out—those who have done good will rise to live, and those who have done evil will rise to be condemned" (John 5:28, 29).

In the Book of Revelation, the apostle John gives us examples of the resurrection of believers. The first concerns the two witnesses in chapter 11, who symbolize believers in the end times who are persecuted under the reign of the Antichrist. "And after the three days and a half [which is interpreted to be

172

three and a half *years* from the time martyrdom be-
gins] the breath of life from God came into
them . . . . And they went up into heaven . . ."
(vv. 11, 12 NAS). The archangel Michael told the
prophet Daniel: "And many of those who sleep in
the dust of the ground will awake, these to everlasting life, but the others to disgrace and everlasting
contempt" (Daniel 12:2 NAS). The people referred
to who awake to this everlasting life are the believers of the first resurrection. All others—those who
reject Christ—are raised to everlasting contempt at
the time of the second resurrection, which occurs
one thousand years later (Revelation 20:4, 5).

Roy Boards the UFO to Immortality

Roy finally discovered *why* he had been drawn to
Devil's Tower: he was one of the select few who
would board the mother craft and journey into the
wonderfully mysterious regions of immortality, according to the gospel of science fiction.

But according to the Gospel of the Bible, at the
time of Christ's return, there will be on the earth
select people—believers—who will have survived
the terrible time of persecution and martyrdom
under the Antichrist. This will be a generation of
believers that will not die! Instead, they will be
given new bodies in a "twinkling of an eye" (*see* 1
Corinthians 15:51) and raised to meet the Lord in
the air at the time of His descent from heaven:

> According to the Lord's own word, we tell
> you that we who are still alive, who are left till
> the coming of the Lord, will certainly not pre-
> cede those who have fallen asleep. For the
> Lord himself will come down from heaven,

with a loud command, with the voice of the archangel and with the trumpet call of God, and the dead in Christ will rise first. After that, we who are still alive and are left will be caught up with them in the clouds to meet the Lord in the air. And so we will be with the Lord forever."

1 Thessalonians 4:15–17

The prophet Daniel wrote about this wonderful mystery many generations before the apostle Paul: ". . . and at that time your people, everyone who is found written in the book, will be rescued" (Daniel 12:1 NAS).

Jesus described it in very clear terms. When He returns, "He will send forth His angels with a great trumpet and they will gather together His elect from the four winds, from one end of the sky to the other" (Matthew 24:31 NAS).

" 'There will be signs in the sun, moon and stars . . . ,' " Jesus prophesied. " 'Men will faint from terror, apprehensive of what is coming on the world, for the heavenly bodies will be shaken. At that time they will see the Son of Man coming in a cloud with power and great glory. When these things begin to take place, stand up and lift up your heads, because your redemption is drawing near' " (Luke 21:25–28).

14

The Coming New World

The gigantic, incredibly structured UFO had landed. Alien beings had disembarked, followed by the missing World War II navy pilots, then a host of other returnees. Not far away, Roy and several other "chosen ones" were being prepared for an incredible journey while, nearby, a priest conducted a strange chapel service for their benefit.

"May the Lord be praised at all times," the priest intoned.

"May God grant us a happy journey," the astronauts responded.

"Lord, show us your ways."

"And lead us along your path."

"Oh, that our lives be bent."

"And keeping our precepts . . . ."

"God has given you his angels' charge over you. Grant these pilgrims, we pray, a happy journey . . . ."

"By the guidance of a star, grant these pilgrims, we pray, a happy journey and peaceful days so that with your divine angel as their guide they may reach their destination and finally come to the haven of everlasting salvation" (Spielberg, *Close Encounters of the Third Kind*, pp. 245–248).

The entire episode—the landing of the UFO, the aliens, the returnees—seemed to give the night a solemn, mystical feeling. And the priest's strange chapel service seemed to give a kind of official religious sanction to the whole affair. It was for Roy an experience of complete peace and a time of reverence and awe. The sheer profoundness of it was nearly overwhelming.

Perhaps this scene originated directly from Steven Spielberg's own personal religious beliefs. "It turns me on," he told *Newsweek,* "to think that when we die we don't go to heaven but to Alpha Centauri, and there we're given a laser blaster and an air-cushion car."

The Coming New World

Is that where we all go when we die? Or is this only Spielberg's space-age interpretation of heaven? Perhaps we should listen to what the Bible has to say about heaven—which the priest called "the haven of everlasting salvation" and Spielberg sees as Alpha Centauri.

The Bible tells us that one thousand years after Christ returns to reign over the world, the present heavens and planet earth will be destroyed by God, then He'll make all things new (Revelation 21:1, 5). This coming new world is described in the Bible in heavily symbolic terms. Its arrival is pictured as the coming of a New Jerusalem. Here is where we find a fascinating parallel with *Close Encounters of the Third Kind.*

Remember the landing of the mother spaceship; the huge, black shape was more than a mile wide and two miles long. Roy thought the top of it looked like an oil refinery, with its storage tanks, pipes, and an array of lights everywhere. But it looked old and dirty—junky, like some old city or a phantom ship that had been sailing the universe for aeons of time.

This scene is so much like the coming of the New

Jerusalem, that it almost seems borrowed from the Bible. The biblical counterpart is found in the Book of Revelation. John, the writer of Revelation saw, in a vision from God, the New Jerusalem coming down, taking the place of the former heavens and earth. But unlike the dirty, time-worn appearance of the mother spaceship, this New Jerusalem has the brilliance of a sparkling gem! The glory and splendor emanating from this New Jerusalem is far greater than any spectacle we can imagine with our limited human understanding. For this reason, John's description is limited to terms that will at least give us a glimpse of what heaven is really like. Keep in mind that what John recorded in the Bible is what he actually saw. Even he could not have comprehended heaven if he had actually seen it. Therefore, God revealed it to him in terms that he could begin to understand.

Here is what he saw:

Then I saw a new heaven and a new earth, for the first heaven and the first earth had passed away, and there was no longer any sea. I saw the Holy City, the new Jerusalem, coming down out of heaven from God, prepared as a bride beautifully dressed for her husband. And I heard a loud voice from the throne saying, "Now the dwelling of God is with men, and he will live with them. They will be his people, and God himself will be with them and be their God."

It shone with the glory of God, and its brilliance was like that of a very precious jewel, like a jasper, clear as crystal.

The city was laid out like a square, as long as

it was wide. He [an angel] measured the city with the rod and found it to be 12,000 stadia [that is, about 1500 miles] in length, and as wide and high as it is long. He measured its wall and it was 144 cubits [that is, somewhat more than 200 feet] thick, by man's measurement, which the angel was using. The wall was made of jasper, and the city of pure gold, as pure as glass. The foundations of the city walls were decorated with every kind of precious stone. The first foundation was jasper, the second sapphire, the third chalcedony, the fourth emerald, the fifth sardonyx, the sixth carnelian, the seventh chrysolite, the eighth beryl, the ninth topaz, the tenth chrysoprase, the eleventh jacinth, and the twelfth amethyst. The twelve gates were twelve pearls, each gate made of a single pearl. The street of the city was of pure gold, like transparent glass.

Revelation 21:1–3, 11, 16–21

A City of Beauty and Wealth

Now let's delve into the meaning behind this highly symbolic description of heaven. First, to recap what has happened: Jesus Christ will have returned by this time. The old heaven and the old earth, with its wars, plagues, and natural disasters, will have been destroyed and replaced by a new earth, symbolized as the New Jerusalem, built by God of pure gold, pearls, and a colorful array of precious stones.

The wall of jasper which surrounds the New Jerusalem, one hundred and forty-four cubits (1500 miles!) high, is symbolic of the security God will give us in heaven, where all unworthy things are kept out.

" 'For I,' declares the Lord, 'will be a wall of fire around her [New Jerusalem], and I will be the glory in her midst' " (Zechariah 2:5 NAS).

The foundation of this New Jerusalem will rest on a solid rock, which Christ told His disciples was the Church (Matthew 16:17, 18). This foundation is pictured as having twelve parts, each with the name of an apostle inscribed upon it. The Church, which receives its strength through the truth that Jesus is the Christ, the Son of the living God, is so strong a foundation for the Kingdom of God that even the power of Satan and hell will never undermine it (Matthew 16:16).

Accessible to All Through Christ

New Jerusalem is seen as having twelve gates, three on each of its four sides, made out of solid pearls and guarded by angels. If the city had but one gate, we would think that entrance into it would be very limited. But this city has twelve gates, three on each of its four sides, which seems to indicate that the city is easily accessible to all who believe, regardless of the direction from which they come to the city—whether they come from Jewish or Gentile backgrounds; whether their skin is black or white or red or yellow or brown. But keep in mind that the angels who stand at the gates will admit only those who believe that Jesus Christ is the Son of God and have received Him as their personal Lord and Saviour.

" 'Blessed are those who wash their robes,' " said Jesus. " 'that they may have the right to the tree of life and may go through the gates into the city. Outside are the dogs, those who practice magic arts, the sexually immoral, the murderers, the idolaters and everyone who loves and practices falsehood' " (Revelation 22:14, 15).

The main street of this New Jerusalem is made with gold, a symbol of purity. All that takes place on this street will be in perfect harmony with God's purpose. What contrast to our cities' streets! Crime in the streets, rioting, accidents, and death. Vulgar lighted signs entice passersby to wallow in the sins of the world. Ours are streets of lonesomeness, immorality, and wasted lives. But the main street in heaven will be like the temple of God since His loving presence will be everywhere and in everyone!

Eternal Light

"The city does not need the sun or the moon to shine on it, for the glory of God gives it light, and the Lamb is its lamp. The nations will walk by its light, and the kings of the earth will bring their splendor into it. On no day will its gates ever be shut, for there will be no night there. The glory and honor of the nations will be brought into it. Nothing impure will ever enter it, nor will anyone who does what is shameful or deceitful, but only those whose names are written in the Lamb's book of life" (Revelation 21:23–27).

This beautiful, holy place is where believers will spend eternity in the presence of God, adoring Christ, and singing praises to Him. Having received immortal bodies at the time of Christ's return (1 Corinthians 15:53), the inhabitants of heaven will be free from death and the limitations of time.

While all of us have fallen short of God's glory in

this life because of sin (Romans 3:23), in heaven, for believers, ". . . He who began a good work in you will perfect it until the day of Christ Jesus" (Philippians 1:6 NAS).

"And the God of all grace, who called you to his eternal glory in Christ, after you have suffered a little while, will himself restore you and make you strong, firm and steadfast" (1 Peter 5:10).

As incredible as it might seem to us now, a time is coming when "we shall be like him" (*see* 1 John 3:2).

All the things of this world soon end up looking worn out and junky—like the mother spaceship in *Close Encounters of the Third Kind*. But the decay goes beyond the material things of this world: The atmosphere in our cities is tainted by hate, depression, and fear. But happily, for those of us who know Jesus Christ as our personal Lord and Saviour and will spend eternity in heaven, the New Jerusalem will have air that will be filled with God's perfect love, joy, and peace. It will be a place of perfect, eternal happiness. There will be reunion with loved ones who love Christ. It will be a place for rest and a place for service and praise to the Lord, Jesus Christ.

15

Opening the Door to True Immortality

Roy Neary's long, lonesome search had come to its glorious end. His perseverance and faith were worthwhile, after all. In a way that he never would have dreamed, and in a place where he never would have imagined, he found circumstances opening the door to immortality. At least, that is the message the movie's producers would have us believe.

The Return to Reality

In movie theaters across the nation, this scene is repeated over and over again: Roy Neary boards the mother spaceship and blasts off into immortality in some untold corner of the universe. As the aliens' craft disappears among the stars, the movie's production credits begin crawling across the screen. Even while the credits are rolling, the house lights come on. The audience—only a few at first, then everyone—begins to stand up to leave the theater. It is strangely quiet, like the end of a solemn church service. It's almost as if the audience were really a "congregation" which has just heard a moving sermon.

Slowly, quietly, people file out of the theater. Some into the darkness of night, others into the brilliance of a midday sun. Regardless of the time of day or night, they have returned to the real world.

For many, the real world is one that keeps them from realizing their true potential. It is a world that dampens dreams and quenches the stuff of life it-self. One wonders about immortality. Certainly, the hope for it does not lie in an everlasting existence in *this* world! There must be a better world, a new world coming.

The Choice Is Ours

We are confronted again with a choice: Are we to accept the gospel of the new space-age religions, or does the Gospel of Jesus Christ remain true?

We are a skeptical people, we Americans. We have invested our people and wealth and time in building a technologically elite society—the first one of its kind the world has ever known. We forged roads through uncharted lands and transformed the wilderness into cities. We wired our buildings for electricity, and spanned the country with telephone wires. Our influence was felt around the world. Now, we are stretching our technological arms to the stars. We are walking on the moon, probing other planets, and are about to send space shuttles alongside comets. But, like the mother spaceship in *Close Encounters*, we are beginning to show signs of age and poor upkeep.

We have fed our bodies to the point of obesity. So, too, we have become gluttons for knowledge; yet we starve from lack of wisdom.

The world promises to liberate our spirits through an all-too-rich diet of secular humanism. And, yet, there is a growing worldwide hunger for God—a hunger for His love, for His forgiveness, and for His guidance in life.

Maybe you are experiencing this hunger for God. Do you have any of the symptoms: loneliness; lack of purpose; boredom; fear; hate; envy; unbelief?

184

Have you been looking to the things of this world for a cure? Has the world taken away your loneliness? Has the world given you meaningful purpose in life? Has the world given you peace, happiness, and joy? Such wonderful things are attainable, waiting for you to partake of them. How? Listen. I've got exciting news for you!

The Gospel of Jesus Christ is not obsolete! It is *true!* There really *is* a God in heaven! He *loves* you—yes, *you!* And He wants you to have a full, meaningful, joy-filled life. He wants you to spend eternity with Him in heaven, in the New Jerusalem. He is standing at the door to immortality, waiting for you to open it and let Him come in to give you the free gift of eternal life.

How can you know this is true—that He loves you? He proved it by sending His only Son, Jesus Christ, to the cross of Calvary: "For God so loved the world that he gave his one and only Son, that whoever believes in him shall not perish but have everlasting life" (John 3:16).

Jesus, in His own words, tells us what He came to do: ". . . I have come that they may have life, and have it to the full" (John 10:10).

Do you understand what this means? The incredible truth of it? Jesus came to take *our* place on that cross so that we wouldn't have to pay for our sins. He paid the penalty for us; we're *free!* When I say "we" I mean, of course, all who, by faith, receive Jesus Christ as Lord and Saviour.

Being free from the penalty of sin is only part of what Christ has done. He has restored the believer into fellowship with God. This has two aspects. First, it means that believers have eternal life and that when Jesus returns, they will receive their new

185

immortal bodies. Second, it means that believers have a new *quality* of life—right now, here in this world. Because believers are children of God, indwelt and empowered by God's Holy Spirit, we can experience today living a life of meaning and purpose.

The Only Way

Jesus said: "I am the way—and the truth and the life. No one comes to the Father except through me" (John 14:6). Only Jesus can restore our fellowship with God, fellowship that was broken by wrongdoing, which the Bible calls sin. And we're *all* sinners: "For all have sinned and fall short of the glory of God" (Romans 3:23). God created us to have fellowship with Himself, but we chose to do our own thing, to go our own way—against God's will and His *perfect* way. As a result, natural man is spiritually separated from God; that is, spiritually dead: "For the wages of sin is death, but the gift of God is eternal life through Christ Jesus our Lord" (Romans 6:23).

Natural man is continually trying to reach God and enjoy a full and meaningful life through his own efforts—living a moral life, adhering to some inadequate philosophy, or holding on to some hopeless religion. But Jesus Christ stands alone as God's *only* provision for sin. Only through Christ can you find a full and meaningful life. Only through Christ can the beautiful door to true immortality be opened.

Jesus has done this by dying for our sins. He rose from the dead, demonstrating His victorious power over death (*see* 1 Corinthians 15:3–6). That same resurrection power is available to all of us. Through

Jesus we can share in His victory over death. There is no other way to pass into true immortality than to open our lives to Christ. He is the only way to God. We must receive Him as Saviour and Lord.

Jesus is standing at the door to immortality: "I stand at the door and knock," Jesus says. "If anyone hears my voice and opens the door, I will go in and eat with him, and he with me" (Revelation 3:20). By opening that door and inviting Christ into your life, you will become a child of God (John 1:12). This door can only be opened by faith. You can only open it by believing that Jesus will come in as He has promised.

The apostle Paul explained that becoming a true Christian is not a matter of how good we are or what we do to please God, but it's the attitude of the heart that counts: "For it is by grace you have been saved, through faith—and this not from yourselves, it is the gift of God—not by works, so that no one can boast" (Ephesians 2:8, 9).

Now, it is not enough to agree intellectually that Jesus Christ is the Son of God, and that He died for your sins. An emotional experience will not open the door to immortality, either. To repeat, the door can only be opened—you can only receive Jesus Christ—by faith. You must *want* Jesus to be your Saviour and the Lord of your life.

Is this what you want for your life? Do you want Jesus Christ to be your Saviour and your Lord? Do you want Him to give you a full and meaningful life? Do you want Him to open the beautiful door to true immortality and receive from Christ His free gift of eternal life?

If you do, then I urge you to express this by repeating the following sample prayer:

Jesus, I believe You are the Son of God. I confess that I am a sinner, and I ask for Your forgiveness. Thank You for dying on the cross in my place so that my sins could be forgiven. Now I open the door of my life and invite You to come in to be my Lord, and to make me the kind of person You want me to be.

Did you say that prayer—and really mean it? If so, then Jesus Christ has come into your life, just as He promised! He has forgiven your sins. He has given you the free gift of eternal life.

The Bible tells us, God ". . . has rescued us from the dominion of darkness and brought us into the kingdom of the Son he loves, in whom we have redemption, the forgiveness of sins" (Colossians 1:13, 14). ". . . God has given us eternal life, and this life is in his Son. He who has the Son has life; he who does not have the Son of God does not have life. I write these things to you who believe in the name of the Son of God so that you may know that you have eternal life" (1 John 5:11–13).

Welcome to the family of God! You are a child of the Father Almighty. You have just experienced the greatest encounter of all time—a close encounter of the infinite kind, that will continue forever and ever, without end.

Response Form

Please fill out this form and mail it today for free literature about the Christian life. (You are under no obligation, whatsoever.)

_____I have just invited Jesus Christ into my life as Saviour and Lord and would appreciate more information on how to experience an abundant Christian life.

_____Please send me more information on how I can become a Christian.

_____Please inform me of other materials for Christian growth.

Name _____

Address_____

City _____

State_____Zip _____

Address all correspondence to the author:
> Frank Allnutt
> P.O. Box 5049
> Blue Jay, CA 92317

WHAT DOES THE BIBLE SAY ABOUT THE
END TIMES?

Don't You Think You Should Find Out?